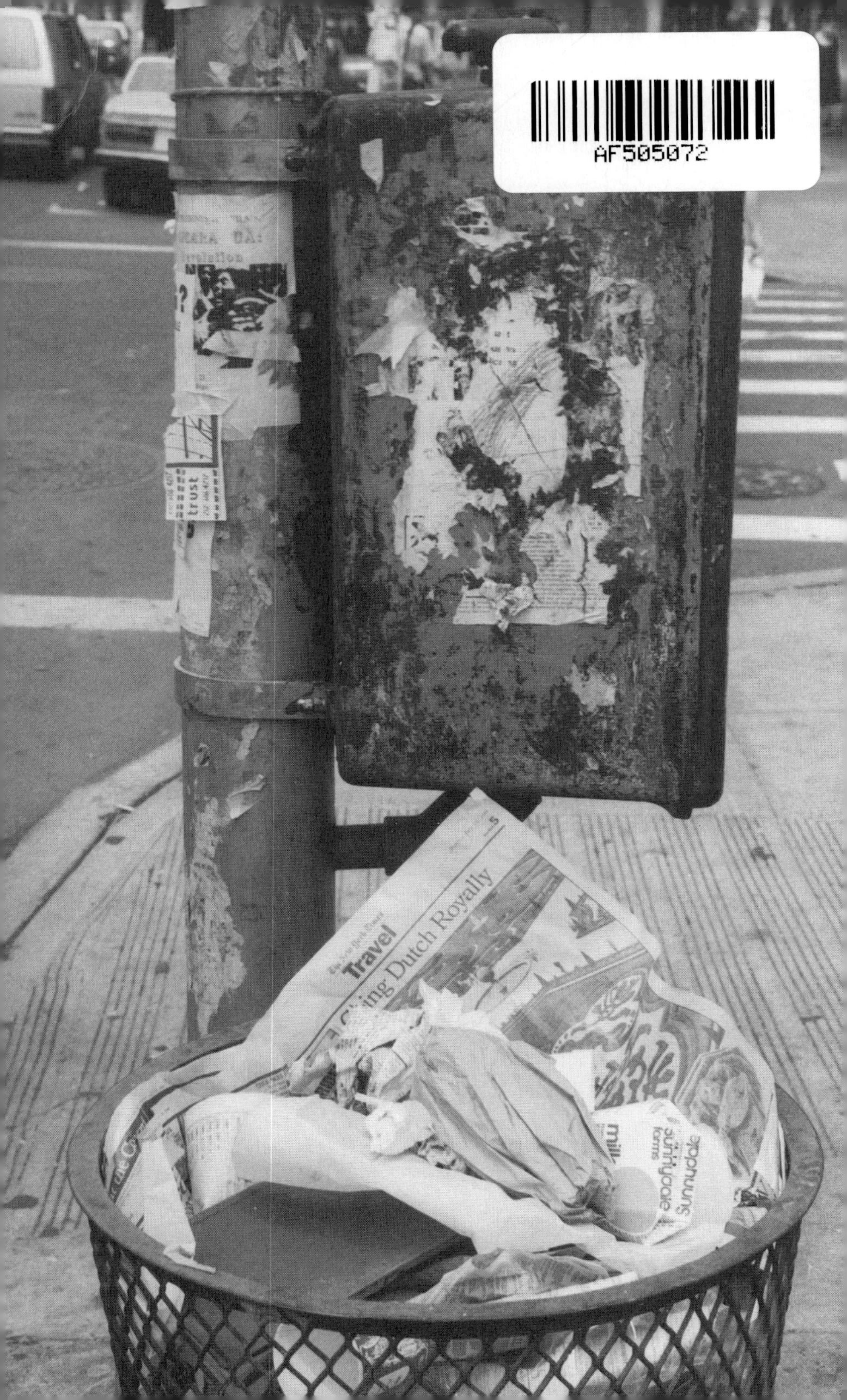
AF505072
trust
Travel
Flying Dutch Royally

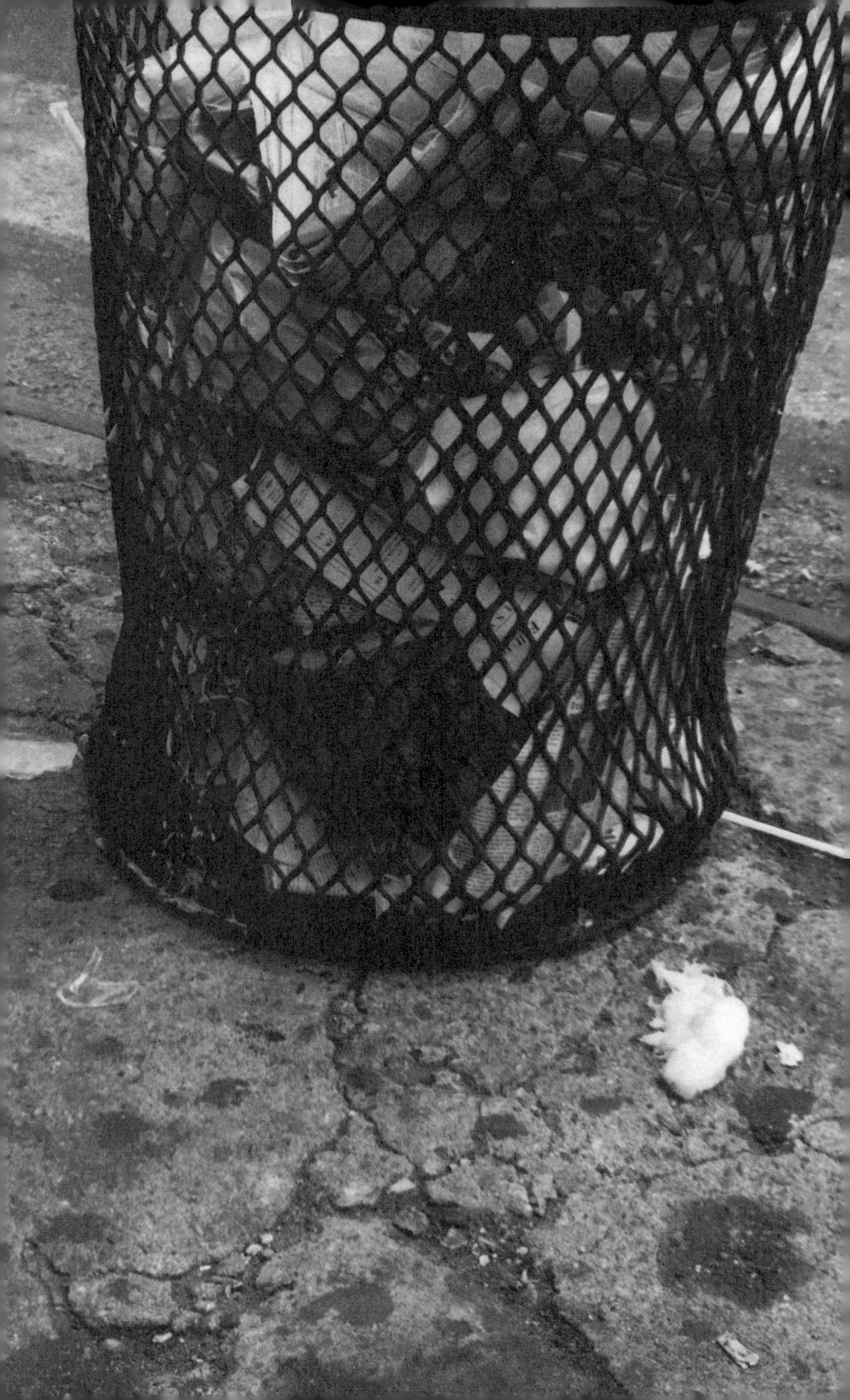

THE TYRANNY OF THE DETAIL

Contemporary Art in an Urban Setting

James Beck

WILLIS, LOCKER & OWENS—NEW YORK

Photographs © by Lawrence Beck

Printed in the United States of America

Willis, Locker & Owens
71 Thompson Street
New York, NY 10012

Library of Congress Cataloging-in-Publication Data

Beck, James H.
    The tyranny of the detail: contemporary art in an urban
setting / by James Beck.
        p.   cm.
    ISBN 0-930279-19-0 (hard : acid-free) : $19.95. —
ISBN 0-930279-20-4 (pbk. : acid-free) : $9.95
    1. Art and society—History—20th century. 2. Art,
Modern—20th century—Psychological aspects. I. Title.
N72.S6B38 1992
701'.03'09045—dc20   92-6779
                                                      CIP

COVER: Photograph by Lawrence Beck

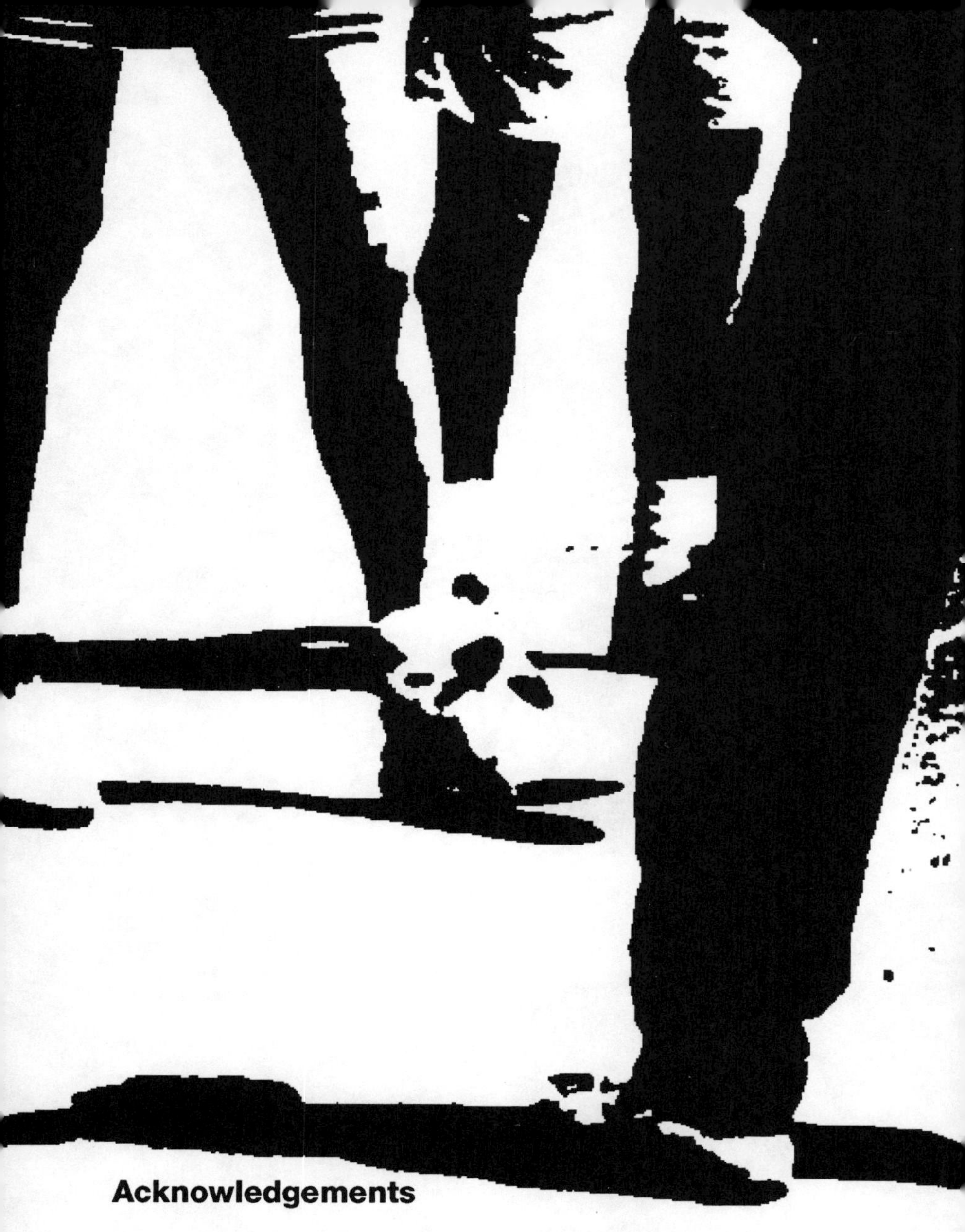

Acknowledgements

I wish to thank Maurice S. Luker III whose reading of the manuscript at the last stages was much appreciated. At an early round, my friends David and Vicky Tabbat did the same thing to the benefit of the final result. Special thanks go to the people at ComputerEase whose editing and typesetting were invaluable in pulling together the whole. Gratitude must be directed to my publisher, who with good humor, creativity and enthusiasm has taken over the project.

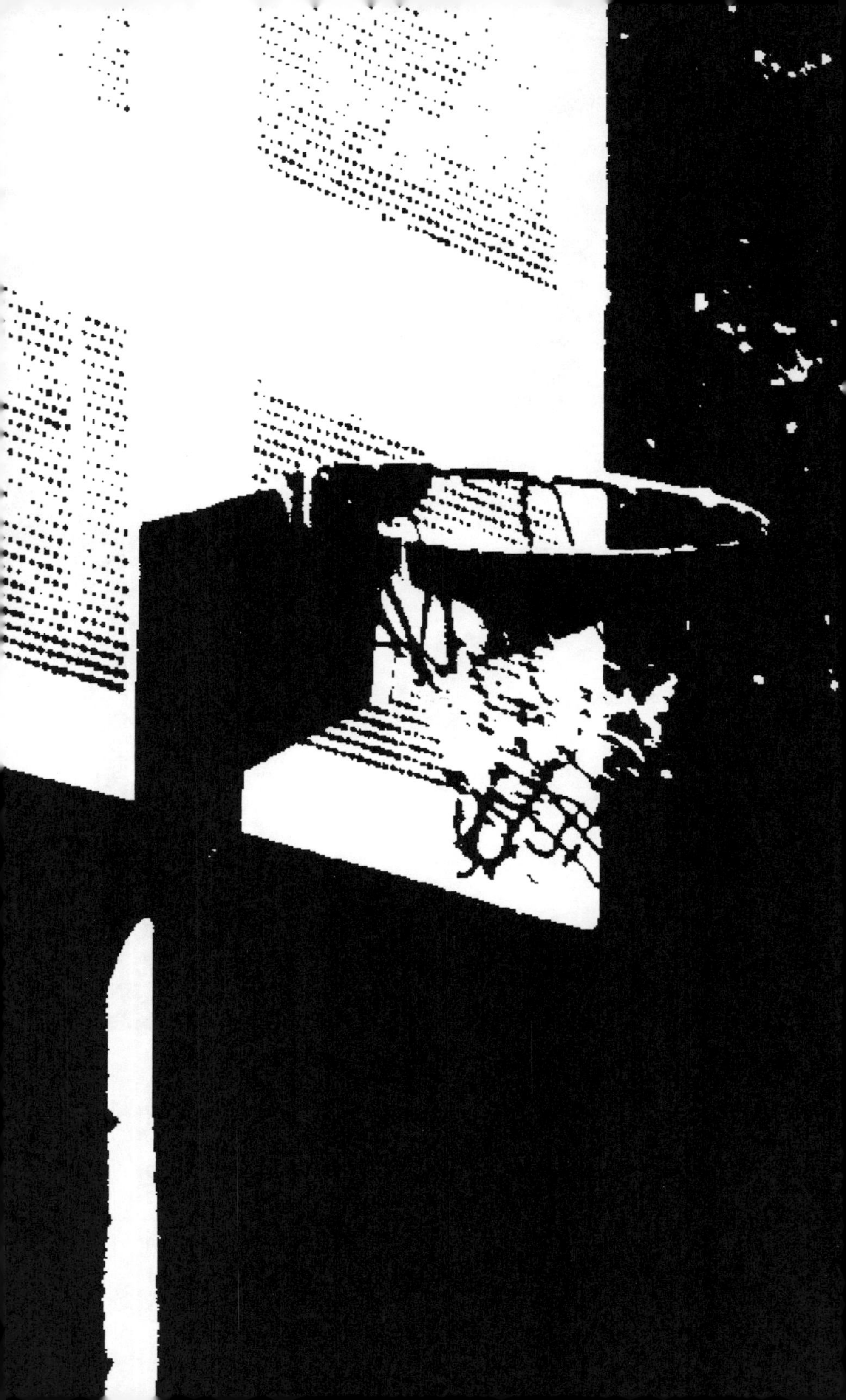

Contents

"A painter paints with his brain, not with his hands."
Michelangelo Buonarroti

Introduction
Purposes and Premises

Successful mainstream contemporary art, by which I mean artworks prominently displayed in luxurious exhibitions accompanied by weighty, multilingual catalogues on glossy paper, examples which constantly appear in the most distinguished places with prestigious commentaries, makes me uneasy. These highly regarded paintings and sculptures have proved to be increasingly perplexing, thereby intensifying a presentiment about precisely what the entire enterprise of art, over and above the actual object, means and how properly to relate to it. Nightmares of that much-abused emperor with his invisible clothes or about houses of cards persistently have surfaced in my thoughts. The puzzlement is especially acute while attending an international exhibition or when I leaf through the more progressive art publications whose influence far outdistances their circulation. Convinced I am not alone in my wonderment, I have set out to explore the situation in the face of the disillusioning realization that few fundamental questions I pose are even being raised in places where one might expect to find them.

Apparently, the influential critical machinery tends to sanction as given what is presented to it in SOHO and Fifty-Seventh Street, MOMA, the Whitney, the Guggenheim, MOCA, in Flash Art and other flashy periodicals, and takes as its starting point a lofty platform from which it analyzes and qualifies, accepts or rejects, praises or damns, but only rarely seeks to test the strength and validity of the foundations on which the whole edifice rests, not to mention the geology of the bedrock underpinnings. To be sure, I have no intention of bashing contemporary art as such or any specific branch or direction, an ungracious activity that would run counter to both my temperament and purpose; rather, my intent is to understand and explain it. Furthermore, I firmly believe that upholding the freedom of action of all artists in whatever course they might wish to steer is imperative for the vitality of art in the largest sense, the artist's creativity, and the health of the culture from which it derives and for which, after all, it is destined. We have even in recent times witnessed situations in which art was totally controlled, and the results, whether in Nazi Germany or Stalinist Russia, have been sterile at best. We have also witnessed the downfall of these tyrannical regimes, awed by the rapidity with which these dramatic changes have taken place. The Berlin wall, like those of Jericho, took only a few hours to come tumbling down.

There might be a sub-issue here too, concerning public sponsorship of art and whether public funding should be available for all, indiscriminately. The political and intellectual establishment has every right, I believe, to choose what it wants to nurture and what it might prefer to reject, provided the decision-making is conducted thoughtfully and fairly. The risk that society might make poor and unsophisticated choices, as sometimes occurs in other areas from ecology to public medicine, cannot be dismissed. Decisions might unjustly advantage some, while what certain experts might designate as less qualified or less original would go begging. Such are, of course, the risks of a democracy. Yet, an artist does not and should not require government (or foundation) sponsorship, as a necessary condition for his creative existence. If sponsorship comes his way, all the better; but at the risk of sounding romantic, I suggest that he should produce his art independent of the funding. If a modern Vincent Van Gogh were rejected for a NEA grant, would he quit painting or abandon the sunflowers simply because it failed to catch the imagination of a jury who might find him too naturalistic, or not naturalistic enough?

Nor should arrived artists be singled out for special attack simply because they have achieved the approbation of a faceless, soulless art establishment. Undeniably, their position makes them particularly vulnerable, much like a highly paid NBA star center, who if he experiences a couple of mediocre seasons on wobbly knees, is subjected to merciless abuse from the same press that had helped pave his way to glory. On the other hand, the most visible artists of the moment need not be heaped with special favors either, merely because they have arrived at a popular and financial success; better let history sift through the complex conditions before pronouncing imperious judgements for eternity.

If anything, my own malaise has less to do with the artists and their activities, good or bad (whatever that really means), famous or not, than with how the pictures the artists produce got to be the way they are, and peripherally, how they are handled by the machinery of art information and by the art market. The troublesome thought arises: a fear that the establishment art complex can adversely affect the very creativity they propagate, in a tail-wagging-the-dog syndrome. The artist can be caught in a maelstrom of events which can cripple his freedom of action and dilute his artistic breadth.

Premises and assumptions lurking behind ideas found between the covers of this book include:

1. As already indicated, I have a persistent sensation that an overwhelming share of contemporary art produced over the past thirty or forty years is of less intrinsic value and integrity than we have been lead to suppose by a well-conditioned, media-oriented art establishment. Although the fundamental issues have little to do specifically with the art market *per se*, "dirty tricks" at the auctions and junk bond tactics, prices and pricing manipulations, public relations agents drumming up publicity, private dealers skirting the edges of the market, will be turned to from time to time when searching for insights that can illuminate the bigger picture. Closer to the heart of the matter still is the necessity of unraveling the visual conditions that permitted or even forced the art to take the forms that it did.

If the art market is not the art, it is nonetheless symptomatic of events surrounding art in contemporary society. The prices do say something about the buying of the public's taste. Paintings by, say, De Kooning, Pollock, Guston and Motherwell and in particular their successors of the next generation, Warhol, Twombly, Johns, Rauschenberg and Lichtenstein, have fetched figures that frequently exceed the million-dollar mark, surpassing levels paid for most old masters that have come up for auction at the same time, in a powerful affirmation of the present. The fervent acceptance of the reality and relevance of our own moment and, conversely, the distancing of the past, are operational notions espoused by contemporaries in culturally authoritative positions.

While one should not confuse the art market with the art over the short run as a reliable gauge to quality, originality, artistic power, or the essential meaning and power of cultural artifacts, nonetheless the realization that say a top international dealer can claim for a collage by a Robert Rauschenberg hundreds of thousands of dollars and even millions if from the "right" period, cannot be reassuring, even to Mr. Rauschenberg. The totals for a single object easily represent the earnings of an excellent artisan for a full decade or the total compensations of capable, sincere, dedicated and original painters or sculptors derived from selling their works over an entire lifetime. Many, indeed most of them, have been forced to earn a living by another endeavor, possibly selling life insurance, real estate, waiting on tables, modelling ceramic bells, or teaching art. In other words, they are locked into activities that erode precious time away from the studio and from their creative enterprises, while their super-successful counterparts not only have the luxury of working constantly on their art but tend to employ teams of assistants to help them produce it. The proportions, in other words, are out of whack, the scale is devastatingly distorted.

The reality that a picture by a publicly celebrated and prosperous younger artist, a Julian, Jeff, David, Francesco or Eric, is worth literally a hundred times or a thousand times, or even ten-thousand times more than a picture by an unacclaimed artist is, frankly, difficult for me to endorse. Nonetheless, such is the net evaluation on the basis of standards that we tend most commonly to apply: money and reputation, in themselves closely tied together in a public–relations–dominated environment. I am aware that Raphael could demand greater compensation than Sodoma in the Rome of the early sixteenth century, but how much? Perhaps one-and-one-half times as much? Titian was paid more than Paris Bordone, as he should have been, but undoubtedly not exceeding twice his rate; and Rembrandt really did not have such a bad time of it, notwithstanding a persistent fiction to the contrary. The current situation seems to be excessively out of kilter, so much so that an exploration is demanded, one that requires a *tabula rasa*, at least as close as we can get, perhaps with a few left-over crumbs from Clement Greenberg and several rings from the coffee mugs and beer cans left behind by Thomas Hess and Harold Rosenberg.

None of what I have suggested thus far precludes the well-documented truth that in the past what turned out to be the most powerful statements of an epoch or a generation were often treated with disdain or even outright neglect by establishments, whether in Paris during the second half of the nineteenth century or in Holland of the seventeenth century. We cannot lose sight of the possibility that certain virtually ignored individuals eventually may be vindicated as more creative, more representative, and more influential than the currently recognized chief representatives of current art.

2. At the core of my ruminations is the assumption that art is a good thing for modern society, essential for that matter, and that artists contribute to the well-being of the culture to an extent that far outdistances their actual numbers. Or, putting it in reverse, without the free-spirited imprint of artists upon modern life, we would all be much the poorer, perhaps even suffocating from lack of spiritual oxygen. I am not referring exclusively to the celebrated inventors who have forged unforgettable images, new movements and new styles, their roles are self-evident. Rather, I am equally concerned with the vast community of practicing artists, mainly trained but not necessarily, who work regularly and honestly producing objects which are perceived as relevant statements by the powers that be. These individuals, numbering in the hundreds of thousands and perhaps even spilling over into the millions in the United States alone, are persistently ignored, in spite of a lifetime of activity. They unwantingly and unwittingly fill the vacuum in our social landscape vacated by the decline in moral leadership that traditionally had been supplied by clergymen, lawyers and judges, philosophers, statesman, scientists and academics.

Artists, often isolated and alone, insistently have been producing, looking, exchanging, for the most part without meaningful monetary reward, crying their cries in the wilderness and singing their songs to the wind for all of us. In this sense at least, I find that both the so-called "good" along with the so-called "bad" artist, whatever measuring yardsticks we might choose to apply, are essential for the health of social structure. Furthermore, at least on this level, the artists as a community or a subclass are all more or less of equal consequence. Both the good priest and the not-so-good one say Mass and hear confession. Thus, I find it offensive that in the cold, absolutist conditions in which artists find themselves, they are savagely assessed without a second chance or mode for appeal. Somehow and somewhere conclusions are reached about who is acceptable and who is not. They must acquiesce for the greater good, and the vast majority end up being discarded in the official labyrinths. The status quo requires revision.

A day's labor has to be something of a indicator, or a week's, or a month's. These are distinctive, measurable and comparable fractions of a lifetime, identical for the arrived artist or for the unsung one. To me it is obscene to completely dismiss as essentially worthless the overwhelming majority of practicing artists out of hand. The awareness of this situation has encouraged me to seek to determine how the conditions in which we are daily participants got that way, ultimately with the goal of seeking remedies. I cannot say I have never met an artist I did not like, but can, at the risk of sounding incurably sentimental, claim that I have never met an artist whose activity I did not respect.

3. The machinery of producing, exhibiting and exploiting art has undergone a drastic evolution over the past generation or so, similar to other changes that have unfolded in modern, especially American, life and more generally life in the West. Artistic careers, like the careers of actors, athletes and futures investors, reach their apex at a much earlier age with less struggle than was the case among artists belonging to the immediately preceding generations, whose expectations, one should add, were quite different. Their goals were rarely outright wealth; they sought freedom to work—the verb artists inevitably favor—to produce, to buy canvas and colors, to think and ponder, to travel, to read, to go to the movies, to exchange views in Cedar bars with other representatives of the arts. Not that they did not also seek exposure and the possibility to communicate, which after all has to be a fundamental aspect of art. None of what I have just suggested means that Picasso, for example, did not make a great deal of money or that he did not enjoy making and spending it. Or that Jackson Pollock did not do reasonably well with sales during those last (few) years before his early death. But being a painter in the past century (and surely much longer than that), was a sacred calling, relatively uncolored by expectations of making big bucks alone, although decent fortunes were nonetheless derived from the activity in every epoch. Artists since the industrial revolution have tended to be grateful and even a bit surprised to be able to survive on their art, perhaps only with an occasional compromise here and there: a portrait one may not have painted by choice, a few private lessons, spending boring hours at dinner parties, accompanying a grotesque dowager through the calles of Venice to open the way to sales.

With the emergence of the Pop generation, substantial amounts of money seemed readily available if all the appropriate ingredients were thrown into the pot in the right measures. Of course, the art had to be "right," that is, engaging to the establishment and having the proper packaging, public relations, the right gallery, the fashionable critic, the most informed collector; all of these factors seem to have been and continue to be, I suggest, part of the formula that leads to status in the current landscape. Success in these conditions has had no bounds and some artists have become newsworthy public heros and the subject of gossip columns and society pages of dailies and the new yellow press, those shabby weeklies sold at supermarket checkout counters across the nation. With such examples as the pilot, still younger artists are seduced from the path of righteousness into seeking their places in the sun quickly, their fifteen minutes, their mention in *Time* Magazine. An ancient Italian proverb has it that every dog wants to piss on the wall. Perhaps nothing in the sorry mosaic is more lamentable than to notice that at the art schools, second-and-third year students are already thinking of the big career, big money, and stardom as they search for an indelible, readily identifiable style.

I am thus faced with a search to explain what went wrong, if indeed something really did go wrong. Obviously many, perhaps most, among the interested art public believe that what occurred and continues to unfold is natural and appropriate. This much I can admit:I do not.

4.   Coming to the material of contemporary art from a heavy immersion in the Renaissance, I see myself at once as freer and more ignorant than specialists in the modern/contemporary material, critics who have been on the scene, pounding the pavements of Soho and the East Village, visiting the studios climbing up the rickety, sharp stairwells, who have contributed to the critical mass of reviews and essays, prepared the catalogues and monographs, who have been in the daily fray for decades. On the other hand, I have had direct contact with oil paint and linen canvas in the distant past and the smell of turpentine in a studio still turns me on, and I have managed to follow the movements as they came and went from the early 1950s onward, although not always with the intensity nor with the care that I might have.

The Renaissance specialization offers useful lessons in how individual lives and individual careers operated and how a single person could and did contribute enormously to an ever-expanding artistic horizon. While the cultural climate had its general impact, it is safe to generalize that a Brunelleschi, a Donatello, a Masaccio was virtually inseparable from the entire fabric of life in Renaissance Italy. Furthermore, for Renaissance art all aspects of the culture, at least under optimum conditions of study, need be delineated. A significant number of artists active in the fifteenth century, especially in the main centers, were first-rate by any standard of measurement, and almost every participant was, at the least, qualified. Having a relatively limited experience with more contemporary events has allowed me to remain free of the jargon of critical writing on the subject, permitting the avoidance of assumptions that may be inherent to the trade but not necessarily useful.

I have another advantage, perhaps my trump card, that of being an exact contemporary of the generation I am writing about. My birth and Jasper's differ by a single day. I remember the day after the bombing of Pearl Harbor in the playground of Daniel Webster School and I remember following the battles on large National Geographic maps attached to classroom walls. I attended the same double-feature Saturday matinees the artists did. I listened to swing and had a collection of 78s, witnessed the emergence of Elvis and the Beetles as they did (on the Ed Sullivan Show), marked somewhat ingenuously the rise of Rock 'n' Roll, was aware of, and frightened by drugs, couldn't resist Johnny Cash, and probably dressed and ate in a similar manner. We all suffered in unspecific bewilderment over the Korean War and definitely felt out of step with Vietnam and suffered the disappointments that the entire country did as the by-product of an unjust, or at least irrelevant, war. We as a nation seemed to have given up being the good guys. I remember when the New York Yankees were unbeatable, just as the US Marines were, and I remember when the Brooklyn Dodgers moved to California. I confess that I did not like Ike much, favoring the irresistible Stevenson from Illinois all the way to two smashing losses, and I recall smugly preferring the *New York Herald Tribune* to the *Times.*

5. What does not appear in the following pages is worth specifying. It is not my intention to produce a book that surveys the period of the 1960s to 1980s, covering the artistic high points, the principal artists, the major exhibitions. As an aside, I admit being temperamentally unsympathetic to the official art establishment which appears to be composed of an unholy brotherhood of influential critics, powerful galleries, prestigious collectors, leading newspapers and magazines, and the major museums.

The main movements, Pop, Minimalism, and Op, will not be specifically defined, documented and dissected, nor will their rise, fall and revival (already!) be spelled out. There are handbooks and textbooks that treat the subject adequately and if not, others will have to write them. I shall scrupulously refrain from playing tired games by quoting newspapers and art magazines from those past decades to find quotable quotations that might either show how right some critics were or how foolishly wrong others may have been not to have recognized Andy or Roy right away, or Jaspers, and Cy.

6.   I recognize fundamental pitfalls about writing about art and especially, but not exclusively, those surrounding contemporary art. I know that a discourse on the visual arts should not aim to mirror or to imitate the art by providing endless descriptions of works which, in my experience, make for tedious narrative and boring, uninformative commentary. The alternative is to seek to formulate a series of elliptical conditions and situations that can illuminate or at least converse with the art. Berenson's famous definition of Masaccio as "Giotto reborn" is instructive both in its own inherent, simple wisdom and as a demonstration of the value of the critical process. Of course, BB does not mean that Masaccio imitated Giotto or that Masaccio's frescoes at the Brancacci look like, literally, Giotto's Arena Chapel murals.That would be utter foolishness. With the introduction of mathematical perspective and, even more significantly, atmospheric perspective the world in which the figures of the two Florentine giants, separated by more than a century, inhabited are not comparable. So what then of Berenson's remark and what then of art criticism? The engaging notion has served to open a side door into the very nature of figurative art in general and the art of Giotto and Masaccio, which after all is quite a lot.

7.   What I intend to offer is a reading of the urban environment out of which much of the art of the past generation has been conceived, and with it an analysis of the modes of reception that depict the same period. I suggest that perception has been severely altered from its operation in the more distant past, having been manipulated by the mass media, and it will never be the same. Further, issues of perception and reception, I contend, cannot be separated from the art any more than the physical presence of the city can which is the most determining factor in recent art.

Dellwood
Dellwood
DEPOSIT CASE
Dellwood
DEPOSIT CASE
Dellwood
DEPOSIT CASE
Dellwood
Dellwood
DEPOSIT CASE
Dellwood
HONEYWELL
FARMS INC.

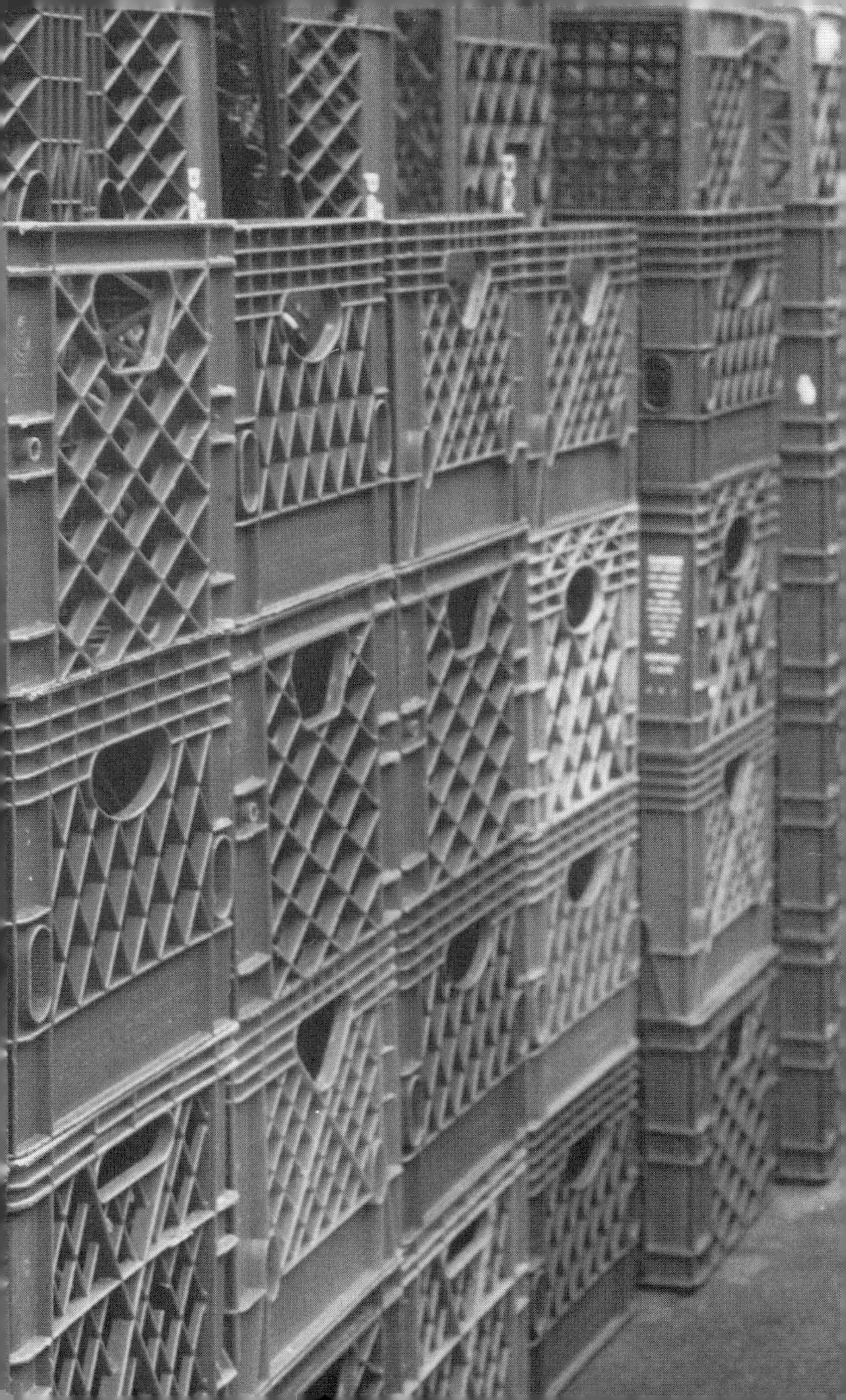

Chapter I.
Generalizations and Background

Several avenues are available to discuss the vanguard painting as well as the sculpture, architecture and design produced since the end of World War II—and, more specifically, during the decades of the 1960s, 1970s and 1980s—whether in terms of movements, styles, or regional developments. The least qualitative and the most innocuous is to view the art of those thirty years as pertaining to a coherent generation. This generation is precisely the subject of my ruminations. The diverse arts, music, poetry, dance, film, as well as the separate visual media (painting, sculpture, design, printmaking, etc.) each have their own clock, ticking away slightly or even radically out of synchronization with each other; furthermore, strict connections with the broader social conditions are never one to one. Innovation seems to proliferate within the dynamics of a particular art form at certain junctures that, in turn, may serve to catapult its sisters onto new paths. The explanation for these organic but unpredictable processes can be traced to the presence of a few or, in certain cases, a single dominating, talented individual who happens to have his home base in a particular area. Such a person or persons can function to advance an entire medium and beyond.

Alternatively, the excitement is the consequence of group chemistry within a discipline where a number of interrelated artists share common goals and formally, or more usually informally, act together to achieve certain goals. Still another mechanism can be isolated in which there is a dynamic interaction between different art media and where one or another set of expressions fertilizes others. Whatever the actual trigger, the extent of innovation may be greater or lesser depending upon the historical moment, the players, and, of course, the standards by which one chooses to measure. While, for example, the fine arts in Italy and Germany during the later 1940s and 1950s might be characterized as being in a phase of treading water — despite recent (politically motivated?) efforts to redimensionalize Fontana, internationalize Alberto Burri, and heroize Joseph Beuys. Creative vitality was burning on low flame in painting, for example. On the other hand, the post-war Italian cinema must be acknowledged for originality of an elevated order, giving rise to a compelling artistic experience, one that ranks with the most impressive attainments of the entire century, whatever art form you might choose, and unquestionably leaving the world of painting far behind.

While Italian (and French) film directors were making brilliant statements with modest means by the late forties and early fifties, in America a new vitality in painting was unfolding, one that appears to have emanated not from a single individual, but from a broadly based, closely knit yet amorphous group of kindred spirits. Sometimes called Abstract Expressionists or, alternatively, Action Painters, what De Kooning, Kline, Gorky, Motherwell, Pollock and the others accomplished cannot be easily defined in simple sweeping generalizations, though by common agreement everyone readily recognizes their contribution.

Innovation and Progress

The scope of this essay is restricted to painting. By mid century, America was in the front line of the battle for artistic innovation in this medium. One should, of course, consider that the border between painting and other art forms has been steadily blurred. The entire discourse depends upon a deeply embedded conviction of "progress." At the least, an insistent, all-embracing pressure for assuming improvement must be accounted for in every discussion of modern and contemporary art. In fact, the specification which has been close to the core of Western art since the Romanesque period, stands at the very foundations of modern art history and art criticism. The search to identify and celebrate the new is constant and tireless: the first application of linear perspective, the earliest use of linen canvas as a support, oil paint, the initial documented application of Prussian Blue, the first mirror depicted in a painting, the first Impressionist or the first Cubist picture, and, of course, as a central topos of modern art criticism—the prototypical collage. As an aside, I cannot resist wondering whether a fragment, a *trompe l'oeil* letter, word or label painted to appear to sit upon the picture plane, counts in the critical exploration, although I doubt that a single critic of modern art would be prepared to award Fra Angelico the honor of having invented the collage.

We are acutely aware of the "progressive" shift in tactics from the Middle Ages to the Renaissance, from the Renaissance to the Baroque, or from Academic to Impressionistic renderings, in which innovative features are regularly understood as winning the constant battle with convention. We tend to read the history of art precisely in this way, achieving gratification when the dreary conventional approach is toppled in favor of a brilliant new one. Even in a fairly unified period (artistically), progress is demanded so that the modest, tentative, soft-spoken style of the early Renaissance is monumentalized into the "high" Renaissance by Michelangelo and Raphael, following a certain fixed course of events. The terms themselves explain the underlying assumption: of course, high is better. But identifying the breakthroughs goes beyond period styles: the subtheme of monographs treating individual artists from Nicola Pisano to Malevich are bent upon celebrating innovations along the path towards perpetual improvement, until wires cross ushering in the inevitable decline, only to be overcome again in the constant process of improvement.

Beyond the accuracy of the identifications, we must be on guard in evaluating so-called firsts to ascertain whether they are truly meaningful, that is, if they have intrinsic value, or whether they merely form part of a conventional rhetoric deeply ingrained in the critical process. Worse still, the "firsts" can disintegrate into a fairly mindless antiquarianism. Yet, how satisfying were those litanies of childhood when the names of the inventors were triumphantly memorized? Alexander Graham Bell—a finely calibrated musical name worthy of a Beatles song—invented the telephone, although the Russians seem to have their own alternate candidate, as do the Italians.

The rarely raised crucial question with regard to the new in art is whether every "first" constitutes an improvement, as is the recognized rule when dealing with engineering or with medicine. For the most part, our (American) orientation inevitably assumes that things are unquestionably "getting better all the time," and they have to or they are somehow getting worse, since the ingrained notion is that things cannot stand still. Think of the rapid expansion of the country itself from those miserable thirteen colonies tucked along the Atlantic coastline. If the GNP does not grow at a respectable rate, if salaries do not improve at least four or five "points" a year, a national crisis of confidence results, and we define ourselves as in a state of recession or worse, depression. When the Dow Jones averages of leading stocks remain unchanged, by common agreement the state of affairs is bad. When home values do not rise at least double the rate of the cost of living, the housing industry is depressed. Who remembers any more that Postal Savings paid a respectable two percent interest in the Depression years? The progress component is tightly woven into the fabric of our thinking, arguably an inherent characteristic of all modern industrial societies. The products offered for consumption seem to illustrate the point best. If television sets do not improve annually, if the automobiles are not made more elaborate with new devices, better gas mileage, more safety features, and all the familiar improvements, we feel uneasy or even betrayed. Something must be wrong, we conclude, and we decide against purchasing.

Tightly bound with the requirement for progress is a related one: products should get bigger and better. Thus, we have the jumbo jet, the jumbo package of toilet tissue (very, very soft), and the jumbo hot dog. The description of measurements has become confusing, but indicative: large dry prunes are really tiny; extra-large ones we might more accurately classify as average, and in real language the jumbos may effectively be large. How big is a "big picture"?

Naturally, artists have not lagged behind other segments of the population.Paintings and sculptures became increasingly gargantuan in their dimensions; they exploded out beyond the measures of private dwellings, sitting rooms and studies, to require especially designed spaces merely to house them. Or, they are conceived for the vast spaces of museums right from the start, rather than traversing a more indirect path from studio to gallery to private collection to museum.

The automobile, that essential measure of American life, was greatly magnified during the decade or so following World War II. As an alternative, the Japanese, following the example of post-war European manufacturers, introduced Lilliputian cars into America, as everyone knows, with remarkable success. Then the imports from the East began to catch the bug, getting ever bigger, so that by the 1980s many Japanese cars were Mercedes-sized.

As an antithesis in the size syndrome, a consistent body of public taste began to prize the very small, mini-things which were assumed to have been engineered with ingenuity. Bigger was better, but so was tiny: mini-radios, mini-TVs, Walkmans, hearing aids, mini-computers, increasingly lighter notebook-like laptops. In the arts, we encounter the giant plastic carrot and the true-to-life–scale Diamond matchstick.

The Pop/Op/Minimalist Generation

The 1960s, 1970s and 1980s were distinct from the trauma of World War II. The preceding period, the 1940s and 1950s, was indeed one of war and its aftermath, marked by earth-shattering political events, especially in the international arena. Wartime saw intensified patriotism: "Remember Pearl Harbor," FDR's "Day of Infamy," "The Yellow Peril," U-Boats and Liberty Ships, V2s and Flying Tigers, nastily efficient Japanese Zeros and very dirty American atomic bombs, gasoline and butter rationing, the black market, spies, the end of the Depression, and finally, the euphoria of victory. The war's immediate consequence, when the Allies split into Eastern and Western blocs, was spectacular industrial and commercial growth in America coupled with an explosion in construction and a staggeringly explosive economy.

In the arts, the post-war period coincided with the onset of a phase of adventuresome probings which, after all, occurred as outer space was being explored. A correlation between the two, the politico-economic-scientific conditions and the artistic ones must be assumed in a society where the arts are integrated or at least where they are not separated artificially from the structure of normal life. When events are especially engrossing, artists necessarily react along with everyone else, and perhaps with greater intensity. An analogy is readily available in the recent breakdown of Soviet hegemony and Communist party rule in Eastern European countries, where one detects a burning, pent-up desire on the part of artists to scrutinize the boundaries of their creativity after forty or more frustrating years of externally imposed individual inhibitions.

Looking still further back to the late 1930s, one finds a noticeable slowdown in all the arts, as if the gears of the potent three-speed Buicks had shifted into neutral to allow the nation's energies to concentrate upon the international ideological and military struggle. The exception was the Hollywood film industry, which it is fair to allege, experienced its golden years precisely in the same period when the "fine arts" were dormant. The explanation for the renaissance of cinema, which has never been considered "art" in the way European postwar film, involves issues beyond my scope here, but what Hollywood produced helped formulate and constantly reinforce the modern American myth and defined the terms of its vision, according to which the art that followed was calibrated. During World War II, Hollywood shared in the war effort with morale building, not to mention propagandistic functions, so that films were not merely permitted, but were encouraged to thrive. And if American visual art in the later 1940s and l950s became an influential export of artistic language, it was preceded by films.

Refugees from Germany and Eastern Europe — artists, writers, researchers, scientists and scholars — participating in every discipline found their way to England and especially America, where they quickly established a rapport with native colleagues. The universal effort was temporarily funneled to the confrontation of world powers. Penetrating criticism and experimentation in the arts were low on any list of national priorities. Still, cranky professors in ivory towers and dogged artists in their dingy studios kept the habit of creative thinking kindled if only on the back burner over a low flame, almost subversively preparing for the new conditions that were inevitably to ensue.

A question indirectly related to the issues discussed is: can art flourish in periods of war or serious turmoil, or does art need a peaceful, stable environment? The Renaissance was, at least superficially, a period of constant upheaval, but war-making activities affected only a tiny portion of the population. Wars were conducted in the fifteenth and sixteenth centuries mostly by professional generals leading mercenary armies, and battles usually occurred in remote places with relatively few casualties, certainly by modern standards. In Florence, for instance, the Medici ruled for long periods, thereby providing stability and continuity. Artists' lives were disrupted in the Franco-Prussian War and in World War I, when promising painters were killed or wounded on both sides. During World War II the U.S. never experienced bombing, strafing, guerilla action, or partisan reprisals. The war was not a time of particular hardship for the population at large: on the contrary, it represented a period of determination, full employment, and strong, paternalistic direction on the political front, plus camaraderie ("Praise the Lord and Pass the Ammunition"), but one in which artistic activity was relatively uneventful.

The comprehensive exhibition of American art in New York City at the World's Fair of 1939/1940 serves as a useful gauge for determining the condition of painting on the eve of total war. The United State's entry into the war occurred only at the end of 1941 and not entirely by choice (although surely by inclination). Europe, while the Fair was still on, was already a battleground. Virtually every entry encapsulated a polite nod to Picasso, to Matisse, or was blatantly regionalistically American. The subject matter manifested in the hundreds of exhibited works, even those by artists like Philip Guston and Adolf Gottlieb, who were to have consequential roles later on and who somewhat surprisingly were represented, consisted in what it had been for some time: still-lifes, landscapes, portraits, figures, and urban narratives.

Had one been forced, following a careful visit through the pavilion there at Flushing Meadows in 1939, to divine the appearance of progressive painting only a decade later, all predictions probably would have been wildly wide of the mark. As it happened, painting as it was known in the past was to be turned on its head in a process in which American artists were, for the first time, pace setters. Nor would the changes that unfolded, above all the shift in the world power balance, the altered position *vis-à-vis* the Soviet Union from ally to enemy, the rapid advances in science and medicine, the invention and actual explosion of the atomic bomb, space exploration and introduction of miracle drugs have been more correctly predicted.

And what can one say in the early 1990s about the state of visual art as we approach the 21st century? We can predict what it will *not* be like by considering the nature of the training young painters are receiving. Artists can move beyond their training, but there are courses, approaches, and choices that are not effectively open to them, unless they take the time to study and learn the necessary tools. Simply stated, you cannot draw the human figure in the manner of Renaissance masters by merely wanting to. You cannot throw yourself into the mysteries of advanced perspective and radical foreshortenings without some sort of preparation, not to mention inclination.

The later 1940s and the 1950s saw a burst of pent-up creative energy epitomized by daring experimentation, by new movements and styles, generally lumped together — imprecisely — as Abstract Expressionism, Action Painting, or the New York School. Analogous if not identical events unfolded somewhat later in Europe, the lag probably resulting from the requirements of physical recovery from the war.

Distinct from America, which never really suffered at all during WW II, but on the contrary actually benefitted in terms of wealth and material possessions, cities in Germany and England and to a lesser extent in France and Italy, required urgent reconstruction. Factories and essential industry had to be put into running condition virtually from scratch. Furthermore, European society with its intellectual class decimated, had to cope with the psychological as well as physical aftershocks of the destruction, and the emotionalism and guilt connected with the war before they could move forward. In the West, especially in Italy and France, robust and highly vocal Communist parties seemed to threaten the very core of the traditional political structure.

At the end of the war, Eastern Europe reflected most of the same circumstances as its Western neighbors, but the situation was quickly and fundamentally altered by Soviet hegemony. A vivid reminder of conditions in Western Europe as it emerged from the war in the late 1940s and early l950s, may be obtained by focusing on Eastern Europe in the early l990s, as these countries and their artists face the challenges of mere survival.

The Supremacy of the Two-Dimensional Experience

The creative terrain had been well mulched during the war period; new plantings took hold quickly once the air cleared and the rains came. The popularity of two-dimensional imagery had been boosted conspicuously during the war. Black and white photography, especially battle photography, published in its effective exponents *Life* and *Look* week in and week out, insistently reinforced the habitualized experience of looking at a flat surface containing page after oversized page filled with vivid, sharply contrasted representations with inherently emotional overtones. The newsreels shown in movie theaters (which were not yet called "cinemas"), like the Pathénews, News of the Week, and the March of Time, had an analogous effect as did Hollywood films which reached classic perfection in the years shortly before, during, and immediately after the war. The war film itself was influential in modifying habits of visual perception. In short, visualizing reality two dimensionally was ever present, reinforcing a mode that dates back to the Renaissance, if not to classical antiquity.

First making its appearance in small, black and white screens and then somewhat later in color, television became a determining vehicle for visual perception by the 1960s. In other words, with still photographs (often exhibiting elevated craft), remarkably accomplished films, and television dramas and reports, displaying reality on flat surfaces either in black and white, or in color with all their illusionistic implications, became a common and repeated visual event. It was a "norm" that must be considered as a basic factor in the modern system of perception, one of

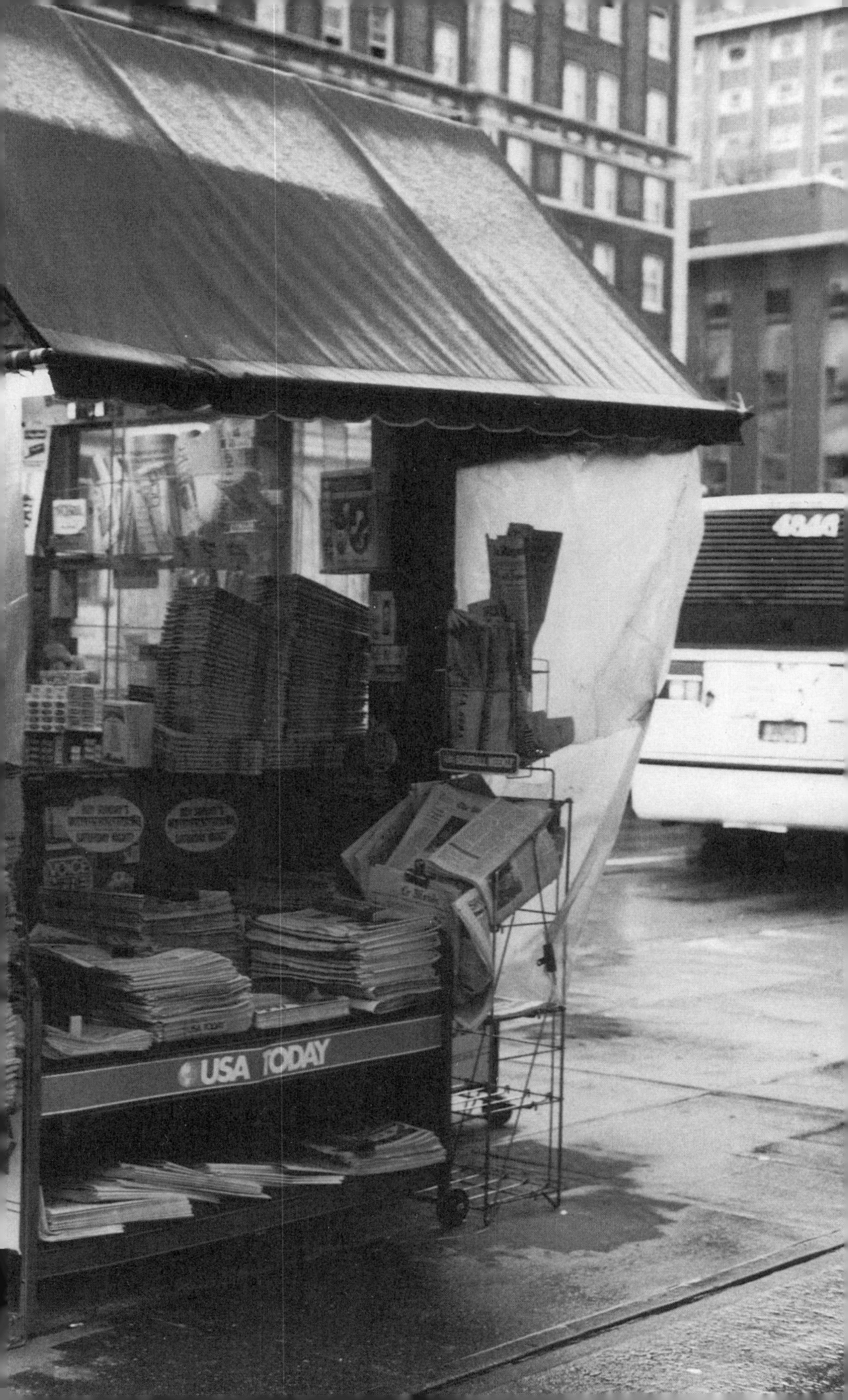
USA TODAY

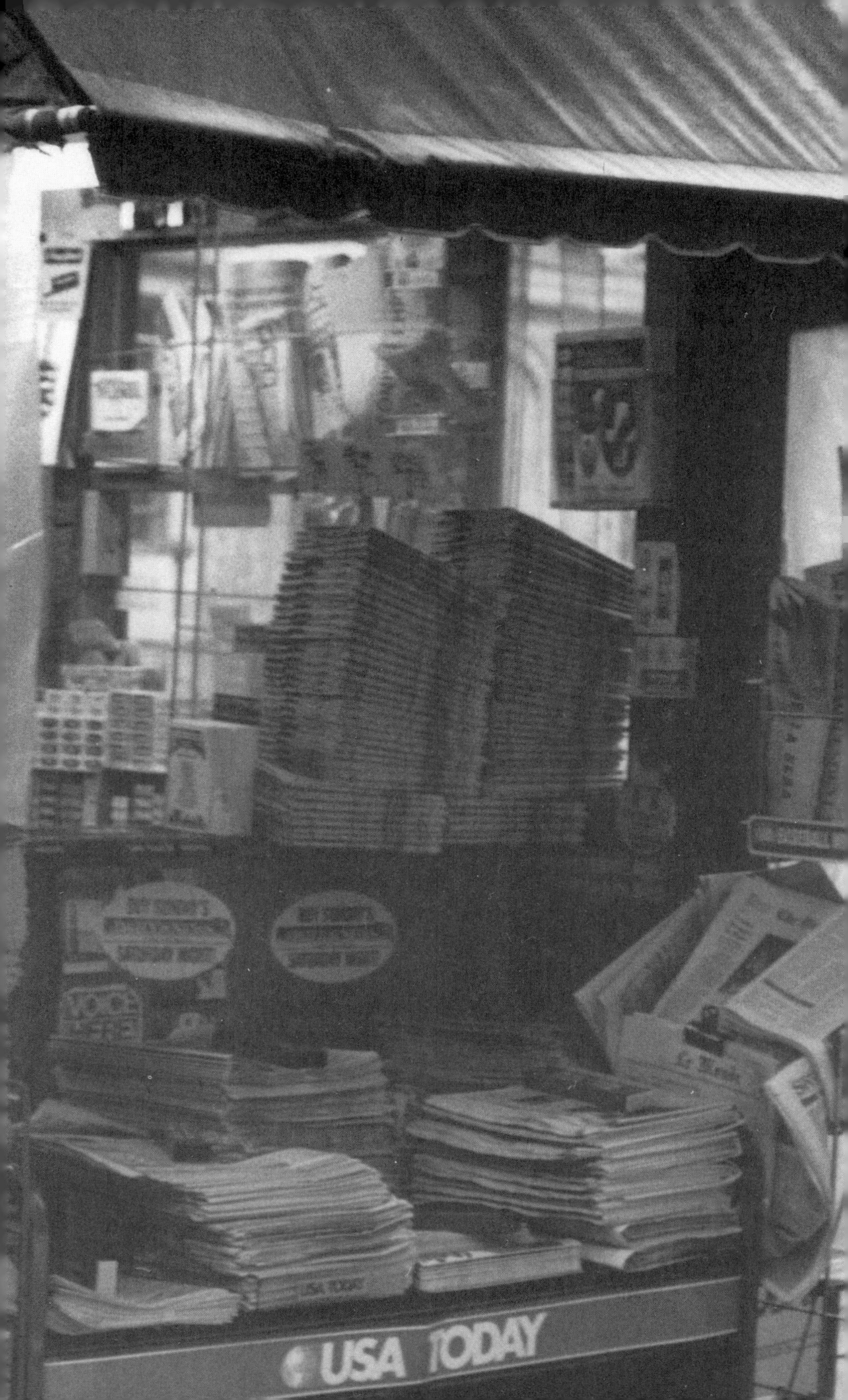

USA TODAY

the most characteristic features of contemporary life, offering a thoroughly alternative experience to past modes of seeing. Nature is seriously rivaled by the "picture," whether still or moving. Furthermore, the awareness that a picture is a translation, an amplification, an interpretation, or a modification of the natural three-dimensional world has become, somehow, nebulized. The two-dimensional evolved into a substitute for, and preferred over, physical reality. In short, the border between real reality and pictorial reality became increasingly blurred. By the 1960s, artists produced their art and spectators observed it under these conditions.

Unlike two-dimensional images on flat surfaces, sculpture in its purest form does not merely imply three dimensions but is actually three-dimensional, requiring that it be comprehended within a context identical to the spectator's space-occupying physicality and the physical world. The perception of painting and its allies—printmaking and photography—which in the Pop-Op-Minimalist generation were effectively merged, inevitably required an intermediary stage between the real and the illusory. In three-dimensional sculpture there is no illusionism, and a transition, whether stated or not, is not a requirement. As might be expected, painting has been far more widely "appreciated" and collected than sculpture in more recent times, simply because moderns tend to be more comfortable with a two-dimensional image than with a three-dimensional one. I suspect that alongside the increased habituation to flat-surface representations, three-dimensional images tend to appear threatening to the individual spectator, since they intrude upon his world, vying with him for breathing room, in a way that painting never could.

To complicate our comprehension of the relationship between the two poles, the real real and pure illusionism, art is often perceived not through firsthand contact but by means of transcriptions in the form of flat reproductions, that is, photographs. When it comes to the reproduction of paintings, there is no loss of medium, but with sculpture the story is quite different. We commonly experience sculpture by means of photographs: its three dimensionality is dematerialized or at least flattened out, and illusionism takes control. In a related transfer, when "appreciating" or experiencing a sculpture or, for that matter, a traditional painting, a portrait, or a religious depiction, the process seems to trigger a chain of visual experiences of other pictures, prints, films, photographs, and dreams: all two-dimensional recollections, skipping altogether reference to space-occupying realities. The point here merely underscores the fact that image as a generic category regulates seeing and, in the longer run, experiencing, and ultimately in perceiving not only art but the entire external world. We are more comfortable relating to nature through pictures or representations of nature, either paintings or, more likely, distorted reproductions of them than when we actually venture into the countryside. The real world's constantly shifting light, color, breezes, heat, humidity, cold, fragrances, bugs, and poison ivy, are effectively canceled out of existence.

This phenomenon needs to be stressed because it directly relates to our perception of all contemporary art, as well as our understanding of the individual in his daily experience of the world. We see and comprehend within an illusionistic set of parameters. Consider for example what today is generically called "signage." A collection of symbols and shorthand marks that offer cryptic instructions of every kind, it reveals to us a continuous language of signs encompassing every aspect of daily life. Automobile travel is virtually dependent upon signs that usually contain a symbol plus a few words or word fragments as explanations, with all kinds of data, even of a life and death nature. Life-threatening situations are summarized by a couple of flat symbols which can be misinterpreted. The power and impact of such signs has not escaped the notice of contemporary artists. In other words, they are not carved wooden or stone totems but surfaces that are comprehended as marks on a single flat, highly readable and familiar plane. Elsewhere, in the workplace and throughout our cities, signs are ever-present impersonal indicators, serving either as attention-getters or warnings. The word, often accompanied by a simplified image or design, surrounds and directs our actions. It is hardly any wonder that the art of the past generation has displayed a particular fascination for the power of the word as image.

The Weight of Picasso and Matisse

Picasso and Matisse have stood as pivotal monuments for half a century and more. Because they were both born long before the beginning of the 20th Century, their chronological ages allowed them to become old masters if not by the 1920s, certainly by the 1930s. Ultimately, they were dethroned in subsequent decades, especially by the end of World War II, as the unchallengeable yardsticks for all that is good, or at least all that is modern in modern art and, to a certain extent, modern life. Their inevitable displacement created a vacuum that younger artists filled. Rather than belonging to the next generation, they were as much as two generations removed from the old suns. The new painters sought drastically alternative formulations, containing solutions that accelerated the unfolding shifts in the reception in art and nature enunciated by Cézanne and by Seurat, rather than the more conventional lessons of Manet, not to mention the more accessible (too accessible?) ones of Monet—surely the most overrated painter in the history of art. Picasso's and Matisse's paintings continued to be for the most part intended for rooms in private homes on a scale that was familiar to the Impresionists' generation, which in itself had centuries of tradition. Among other things, by the mid- and late-20th century the newer artists made a complete break from the more strictly domestic orientation that had dominated previous art.

The dominance of Picasso and Matisse (and there is no denying that they continue, in a historical sense, to hold positions at the top of any list of the finest painters of their age) was seriously undermined by the 1940s and the early 1950s. Nevertheless, being familiar and handy, they engaged a broad public. In fact, the products of their old age were hailed as tokens of unassailable confidence and artistic wisdom. Yet their work offered few insights for viewers and still less for artists belonging to the generation of the 1960s–1980s. They were "classics" like books on the shelves of the New Rochelle Public Library, inevitably on required reading lists, contributions that continue to be consulted and even read out of duty, admiration and guidance but not as sources of fresh enlightenment. Along with Rembrandt, Delacroix and Velazquez, for example, they became less specifically applicable as inspirations for active painters. Cézanne appears to me the notable exception, as he has been for a full century.

The artists who attained prominence after World War II had alternate heroes and other models: Klee, Mondrian, De Chirico, Duchamp. Increasingly receptive to impulses from non-Western cultures (as both Picasso and Matisse were already, for that matter), and like society at large they seemed overripe for drastic shifts. Along with wealth, new power, the New Math and the New Physics, a New Art seemed as appropriate as it was inescapable. America's automobile industry provides instructive analogies. The first cars that rolled off Detroit's assembly lines after World War II, which found an unquenchable public demand, were based upon models conceived on drafting tables before 1941, so that the 1946 and 1947 models were releases of pre-war editions almost to the letter. However, within a few years, cars began to bloat in every dimension. Preposterously winged fenders, contrived and bent bumpers that wrapped around the sides (and were heartbreakingly difficult and costly to repair once crunched) were decorated with two or even three pinks, pastel yellows, turquoise hues. The horsepower doubled and redoubled, with efficiency in terms of gasoline consumption reduced to as little as four and five miles per gallon in the case of fully accessorized models. Low gas mileage became a status symbol, a sign of prestige based on how much one could afford to waste.

Advertising agencies became the *de facto* designers of the new models. Their desirability was artificially inspired in a vicious and ultimately self-destructive cycle, usually on the basis of two-dimensional imagery. The publicists created a demand for a product with a set of characteristics; the manufacturers then produced what was assumed to be legitimately demanded. After a while the advertising assertions became the reality and were frozen into the thinking of designers and engineers. The eventual disenchantment with the American-made automobile, compounded by the declining quality of the new models — too frequently "lemons" — opened the door for the importation of more economical and better engineered European and especially Japanese models. In terms of automotive style, the Japanese unabashedly imitated the European models, but simultaneously they brilliantly incorporated an American taste factor, starting with small, utilitarian, pseudo-sporty models.

Following their colossal success in North America, Japanese automakers introduced a vehicle somewhat awkwardly called the "Yellow Car" in Europe, following an evolution of their own. The American and European manufacturers began consciously to emulate the Japanese imitations, in a dadaistic switch of interchanging influences. The new twist was that Japanese cars began to grow much bigger, more powerful, complicated, Mercedes-like, expensive, and less economical and less efficient, in contrast to their original *raison d'être*.

To return to the arts, vanguard painting in the 1930s was tinged either by diverse cubisms in all their optical and intellectual complexities, with the collage and the use of words and letters, or by the planar manifestations associated with Matisse. Potent progressive impulses from Europe were felt in America through reproductions, with all the inadequacies of size and scale, in the art magazines whose impact deserves careful attention. In addition, art books consisting mainly of photographic reproductions made their appearance in a big way. The unmatched collection of the Museum of Modern Art, where prominent contributions of the Russian modernists and Italian futurists could be consulted along with more familiar avant-garde French and Spanish contributions, was a force of incalculable consequence. During the pre-war and immediate post-war periods, MOMA's impact cannot be overestimated because its holdings of preeminent quality and unrestrainedly original work had been available to American artists and others visiting or living in New York. Indeed, the museum's collection formed the single most influential internal (i.e. art) factor in the evolution of the new idiom as it stormed upon the scene in the late 1940s.

Categorizing and defining a painter by isolating "influences" he may have absorbed from avant-garde Europeans (on display at the Museum of Modern Art) has been commonplace. Attaching a particular artist to one or another earlier period offers only superficial insights into how ideas are passed from one generation and from one individual to another. One may be able to isolate a series of similarities, or even actual specific borrowings. For example, Kline's use of thick black strokes is related to Rouault, but does this observation, if indeed true in the first place, lead us very far in our understanding of Kline's art, or Rouault's, for that matter? Since such observations are reasonably concrete and readily communicable while other more esoteric ones may not be, they have become standard and as such even appear as desirable.

MOMA undeniably had offered otherwise inaccessible examples of the highest quality and broadest range to a generation of artists and critics as well as to an interested public, all of whom were hungry for enlightened inspiration. The immediate impact was to create an awareness of the finest examples from the international world of modern art, one reinforced by illustrated books, postcards, as well as reproductions. Everybody had picture postcards tacked up around the studio. No doubt, these "Museums Without Walls" had an extensive effect. Museums like MOMA, along with the Whitney and the Museum of Non-Objective Art, housed the real thing in living color, in correct scale and with the aura, surface, beauty and mystery of an original artwork. The very act of seeking out the pictures in museums, the effort required by artists to get there, to New York, to mid-town, to their physical presence, the procession through the galleries and the corridors were partly acts of homage and partly religious rituals. In MOMA's temple on 53rd Street, the radiance of the inventions, the documentation of risk taking and of commitment to a sacred activity were passed along like the Olympic flame from those earlier runners to the next generation.

America and especially New York, where a vigorous and unanticipated outburst of originality was unleashed by artists, became by the late 1940s and early 1950s the center of the international art world, as Paris had been before World War II. This assertion, despite its chauvinistic and heady self-confidence, is probably true. In such stirring circumstances, some of the "lesser" artists naturally shone a bit too brightly, given their limited talents, although they benefitted from the whole phenomenon because they were in the right place at the right time. But that was also true of Harry Truman. Such is inevitably the case with movements involving a substantial number of persons. The guiding figures, Pollock, Rothko, Motherwell, Still, Kline, De Kooning, Newman and to a lesser extent Guston, Reinhardt, Gottlieb and Tomlin, were by the 1950s middle-aged, hardly neophytes to galleries and museums. Each of them had, of course, well-defined early phases (Newman and Motherwell were among the exceptions) that were quite consciously concealed, as if the principal parties — the artists themselves, the critics and the galleries — had taken an oath to blot out the past. They camouflaged or actually manipulated history by denying aspects of the past that were in almost every instance characterized by relatively conventional productions in a relatively conventional presentational format, frequently dependent upon impulses derived from Picasso and Matisse. Anything that smacked of conventionality had to be obliterated from their past. If there had been a regionalist background, as was the case with Pollock or, in a different configuration, with Guston, this, too, was swept under the critical rug. The justification for this adjusting of the past seems to have been that the writers who were key spokespersons of the new were unhappy with the thought that their current heroes could be interpreted as being in any manner conventional, even in their youth. The artists were presented as creative from birth, revolutionaries in their personal and artistic *personae*. They had a stroke, a touch, a mark that was exclusively theirs and they had always had it. The galleries happily perpetuated this fiction, which even after forty years remains difficult to undo.

Part of the explanation for this critical deception may be that the war's end seemed to demand a cultural blank slate, one that served as a continental divide between two very distinct social, political and artistic moments. Hence, the strength of the fiction. Somewhere around 1948 or 1950 was really a Napoleonic Year One: everything before was irrelevant prehistory, in an unusual manipulation of history which became history.

Sophisticate or *Naif?*

One of the effects of the Abstract Expressionists' obliteration of their artistic pasts, now sanctified by dozens of MA and PhD theses, monographs and catalogue raisonnées, was to hinder the critical process. The full account of many of the painters in the qroup was not only ignored, but actually hidden. As a result, certain Abstract Expressionists who should be classified as *naifs*, have never been so characterized. Henri Rousseau, the most celebrated *naif* painter in recent times, betrays that aspect immediately. When a painter depicts a recognizable reality including figures, his art is vulnerable to being read as either learned, schooled or *naif*. The conclusion is reached with little difficulty. With abstract and non-objective representations, on the other hand, self-trained painters are not so readily identified. The recognition of conventional skills such as rendering the figure and locating objects in space, foreshortenings and perspective, so familiar from photography as well as from traditional art of the past five-hundred years or more, cannot be applied to non-figurative explorations. Abstract artists, whose need for expression and whose own native ability, inclination and especially native talent, do not stamp themselves obviously as *naifs*, might actually be understood better if we could. Painters like Motherwell, Reinhardt, Newman, and Burri, to name a few, have created works which are brimming with freshness, innocence and openness achieved without traditionally learned mechanics. But since they operated in a non-figurative genre, the separation between professional, that is to say, formally trained painters, and self-taught ones is no longer self evident, as it is in an instant with Rousseau or Grandma Moses. We know that De Kooning had a relatively conventional art school training in Holland and so did Pollock at New York's Art Students League with Thomas Hart Benton while a number of their colleagues in "the Movement" were self-taught. By grade-school standards many, to be blunt, could not draw. Undeniably, it is quite possible that a dreary, conventional training by ungifted, insensitive teachers might have trampled their originality and spirit, and on balance we might have been all the poorer. Yet, I believe that we should be conscious of the two typical avenues to becoming a painter among members of the immediate post-war generation, and also recognize the possible effects that formal training or non-formal training may have had upon them and what followed.

For the next generation of artists, those who merged in the 1960s, 1970s, and 1980s, conditions surrounding art training had changed again . The non-figurative mode was quickly formalized into a teachable approach in art schools, becoming virtually the only one taught, so that non-figurative art became self-conscious, eventually rigid and typically intolerant. Power corrupts.... By means of design exercises, the study of the mark, the gesture, and color experiments, the non-objective approach was legitimized and professionalized. This fact does not preclude, however, categorizing Motherwell as a *naif*, nor, of course, does it suggest that he is not highly skilled and informed in matters of art (in the way Rousseau was?). I raise the issue not to reduce their accomplishments but to define the situation within the framework of historical accuracy. Yet to some extent, the self-taught became the teachers in a somewhat unique turn of events.

Traditional skills and techniques in drawing, in rendering the figure, in modeling, in treating color and form are essentially teachable and have been passed along for centuries in the workshops of artists and in the academies. Given the conditions of the early 1940s, less stress (if any at all) was placed on the formalities, and thus the non-professionally trained or self-taught artist, too, could operate without prejudice. The generation who took their place in the sun during the 1960s and after, did not have the same flexibility. As has the pattern between generations for centuries, they rebelled against the instruction they had received, which was mainly abstract and expressionistic.

New York evolved into (and still remains as these words are being processed on my black and white IBM PC) the international center of progressive art activity as defined by the art market, the museum structure, and the art press. That is, over the thirty-year span that constitutes the center of concentration here and spilling over into the current decade, the 1990's, international world-class art is the art more often than not made, exhibited and sold in or through New York.

Naturally, other centers continue to manifest vital, engaging and intrinsically valid activity, but New York remains the anointed art capital, though for how long is a question. New York City is where progressive galleries are located and where collectors come to purchase avant-garde art. Many who reside in other areas of the country, in Los Angeles, Houston or elsewhere have apartments in New York (written off as a business expense) to attend theatrical performances, the opera season, concerts, and in general to absorb what the city has to offer culturally, but mainly to have a base for their art purchasing.

The Collectors and Their Dealers

The collector's vital function within the total equation that constitutes the mechanics of the contemporary art world should not be taken lightly or for granted. Rather, the passionate art collector as well as the collector-investor has a cardinal position in the total constellation of establishment art in New York City and throughout the world. A holy alliance between dealer and collector cemented during the past few decades continues to define a successful and profitable marketing situation. Informed dealers like Betty Parsons, Samuel Kootz, Sidney Janis, Leo Castelli, Ileana Sonnabend, Mary Boone, and the owners of Pace, have functioned as teacher-advisors to their clients; they are primarily independent, tough-minded American entrepreneurs who have experienced immense success in their business activity. The sociology of grand-scale collectors with their peculiar cultural formation and business-oriented psychology has had a consummate impact upon how events unfolded. The goal sometimes is to create their own museums, as Joseph Hirshhorn did in Washington, D.C.

As pupils of the teacher-dealers, they rapidly became art-educated, and being immensely skillful and worldly individuals in their own areas, they soon began to act with independence where art was concerned. The tables were turned as the newly informed, well-heeled, strong-willed collector of contemporary art began acting on his own and actually influencing the choices of the dealers as the rapport between the two was modified. Early on in the collector-dealer collaboration, the dealer was in complete control, but as time passed, the collector was able to impose his own taste and personality, and the balance shifted. More recently, the collector has had a strident, at times even a commanding, voice that is felt outside the galleries directly by the artists and by the museum world with whom the collectors interacted socially . One might suggest that the situation is hardly different than in times past, when the patron — whether the church, one of its institutions, the prince or the powerful merchants — had substantial impact upon the artist and what he produced. We must examine the cultural possibilities of the new patrons, the collectors, their experience with art on a large scale, and their potentiality for stewardship. Additionally, the mediation of the dealers cannot be taken lightly.

Europe and America

America's hegemonic position in the world, and especially as regards to Europe, coincided with the apparent dominance of the United States in the arts. The country's unprecedented wealth in the decades following the conclusion of World War II as well as unparalleled military power and surging pride at having saved the world for democracy had an enormous impact upon the arts. Wall Street and the New York financial institutions together with the California-based Bank of America dominated the rest of the world (all put together), and what was good for General Motors was good for the country and good for humanity. Through the Marshall Plan, the United States financed the early phases of reconstruction and recovery in Western Europe. America's reputation had never been higher, nor that of its representative products: Virginia tobacco, Coca Cola, Fruit of the Loom underwear, Levi jeans, jazz, Negro spirituals. Great American novels and lesser ones were instantly translated into a dozen languages. Fine art produced in the United States was made available to an eager European public through such structures as the United States Information Agency — which also propagandized films, theatrical and music productions, and other manifestations of the arts. Along with American power, military dominance, and the Yankee dollar came a phase of extensive Americanization felt in every aspect of European society, from its literary vocabulary to its music. The interrelationship between Europe and America in the decades following the war was inevitably a two way street, however, with the new element being a consistent American flavor and sensibility exported in the direction of the old continent. At the same time (and I suggest that this an underappreciated point), America continued to become increasingly Europeanized: one need but consider the change in menus in the American home from the 1940s to the 1980s; and if the current dictionaries of major European languages are filled with Americanisms, numerous European words have entered into regular use in the United States. Political and cultural isolationism were dead issues. Undoubtedly the American expatriate artists living in Italy and France in particular, as well as those back home were keenly informed of the newer European events.

In other words, expatriation served as an influential conduit for the propagation of American culture and art in Europe, but also as a receiving station for all sorts of Continental signals. The outbreak of World War II had effectively put an end to Americans living in Europe, particularly in England, France, Spain and Italy, but once over, the aficionados, joined by the younger generation, returned to favorite haunts, bringing with them a curious blend of an intimate knowledge and unabashed affection for their privileged corner abroad, in Paris, Mallorca, Florence, or Rome. A lingering, heavily veiled, yet formidable bond with home, i.e., "the States," persisted in their thinking, however. While effectively, if superficially, integrated into the fabric of the society where they resided, Americans living permanently abroad continued to have a circle of American or at least English-speaking friends and continued to seek out favorite products, including characteristic foods. One of the most difficult to locate, really impossible, was sweet corn, and determined Americans went to enormous pains to plant their own. The Paris-based *Herald Tribune*'s readership expanded steadily, while other American-style newspapers of dubious value were published elsewhere, including *The Rome Daily American. Time* was a mainline connection with the American point of view for those living abroad, and expatriates listened to the *Voice of America* or *Armed Forces Radio*, at least for the news and to see how many homers Ted Williams whacked for the Red Sox so far in the season.

Among the Europeanized artists, writers, poets, sculptors, musicians, and painters who comprised a respectable portion of the American expatriate population was a category instituted by the GI Bill, a law permitting veterans of military service to study virtually anywhere they wished, including accredited foreign art schools, from Mexico City and Berlin to Rome. Living in Europe, especially in the old centers of art with their unsurpassed museums and honorable artistic traditions, had an incalculable effect upon the younger artists. The public collections, the churches, the *piazze,* the palaces, the bistros and cafes, the *trattorie* and sidewalk restaurants, the scale between individual and place, all left a vivid impression. Institutions like the American Academy in Rome resumed their activities, serving as a conduit between the old world and the new, while the "Rome Prize" was a prize indeed for American artists.

In addition to those Americans who lived in Europe for extended periods of time, hardly a single American artist failed to take some sort of tour, if not the grand one, in the years after 1945, first by ship and then more regularly by plane. The old world was flooded with culturally hungry youth unloaded from the bellies of cheap charter flights, who were joined by hordes of usually overweight, mature tourists clothed in shapeless, brightly colored dacron prints. If it is nearly impossible to measure accurately the extent of the impact of the European experience upon the travelers; could a few sessions in the Prado, the Louvre, the National Gallery, the Uffizi have failed to instill a healthy respect and even awe for ART, resulting in a disposition to visit museums and generally to support culture back home? Those anecdotes spun out with a resounding, authoritative voice in an unimaginable English about Raphael's mistress, Cézanne's mother or Goya's nude and clothed majas, a collection of conventional truths about the art of the past, were an unforgettable element of the European experience. Waves of tourists came, partially motivated by nostalgia and by the desire to participate in the more refined life at a favorable rate of exchange. For the first twenty or so years following the war, Europe was a relative bargain for Americans, who could buy better crafted and more elegantly designed clothing and other items at low cost.

The temporary but constantly renewed presence of Americans in large numbers in Europe surely affected the native population. If the Irish who immigrated to New York by the boatload in the 19th century had to adjust to the city, its habits and its institutions, they, like Puerto Ricans in the 20th century, effectively altered the city to which they had come. In short, the presence of large numbers of usually amiable Americans had a perceptible resonance upon the host countries and host artists. Furthermore, the art that expatriates were producing and exhibiting together with the art that interested them from back home also permeated the European landscape. In sum, the presence of Americans in substantial numbers—artists, students, tourists, retirees — inevitably had a share in the definition of post-war European culture. During and directly following the war, Americans, in the guise of the visible military presence, had a lasting impact upon Germany in particular. For the first time, there could be found a substantial, visible, non-colonial black presence in Western Europe.

While focusing on the American side and what American artists and students might have absorbed in Europe, the reverse of the coin is an often ignored but influential factor. Not only were American works present in abundance but so were Americans, and the conversations in the Parisian and Roman cafes about newer art surely were carefully recorded by both camps, vitalizing artistic conditions and thereby affecting thinking about art.

The Rapidity of Change

After the war, changes in every area of society were as swift as they were extreme, and the arts were not excluded. The most remarkable aspect was the astonishing rapidity with which the changes were manifested and were accepted by the establishment, or, at least, given tacit approval by leading media outlets like *Vogue*, and *The New York Times*. That a magazine devoted to high fashion could have had a significant share in pulling along new, experimental art is sociologically revealing. In fact, the interelationship between the high-style fashion industry and contemporary art is not readily explained but unquestionably exists. Art galleries in SoHo, the Upper East Side and 57th Street share not only the same buildings with exclusive retailers but the same customers. Taste in art and fashion is subject to change at a moment's notice because of public fickleness; it is fair to conclude that the designers and those connected with the fashion industry are quick to accept new art and to apply it to their own activity.

Understanding the New Art

By the time of the landmark Fifteen Americans exhibition at the Museum of Modern Art in 1952, if not earlier, the new post-Cubist, non-objective, non-figurative art had received unprecedented support. Yet, it was rarely understood. This odd condition of having achieved support without comprehension is a basic component that surrounds much contemporary art. One may argue that art was never widely understood in any historical period (which is probably not true), yet the fact remains that for the more recent past the museum-going and art-purchasing public was perfectly contented to participate on simple faith and on astute instinct.

The photograph which appeared in *Life* of 15 January 1951, like a painting from the previous century or the fifth grade at PS 89 in Queens, shows the "irascibles." The mere appearance can be interpreted as symptomatic of the willingness and even the disposition to accept dramatic changes in artistic language. A potent, interested public was prepared to sanction an essentially unfathomable expression with enthusiasm colored by a heavy dosage of naiveté. Represented in the photograph were De Kooning, Gottlieb, Reinhardt, Hedda Sterne, Pousette-Dart, Baziotes, Pollock, Still, Motherwell, Tomlin, Stamos, Jimmy Ernst, Newman, Brooks and Rothko. Since *Life* was unchallenged as the nation's most-powerful mass-media outlet, the inclusion of the photo must be interpreted as an indication of changes in the popular mood, coinciding with the moment when television was awakening from its infancy.

Television, perhaps because of its scale, never proved to be specifically influential for the exploitation of the fine arts, although the effects of television upon modern life and modern perception form the subtext of any analysis of the period.

From the 1960's to the 1980's, New York was the uncontested center of world finance, the capital of the recording industry for classical as well as popular (but not country) music, the home of the New York and the NBC symphony orchestras. Its concert halls were among the most prestigious and the Metropolitan Opera had a world reputation dating back decades, when Arturo Toscanini first dominated the scene from the cliffs of Riverdale. The publishing industry flourished. Modern dance companies together with progressive music, indeed all art forms, found a thriving base in New York City. In the visual arts reputations were created swiftly as a derivative of the increasingly efficient mass media. Artists, in turn, became public personalities in a New York that saw the growth of an entirely new activity, public relations. Who would doubt that Raphael's influential relatives and the Dukes of Urbino, not to mention his countryman, Bramante, lighted his path to Rome? In more recent times art galleries as well as individual fine artists, following the lead of writers, actors and musicians, have retained professional publicists. Most artists in the past and still today, either out of choice or necessity, have done the job by themselves. Others judged it imperative that the amateurishness be taken out of career building, and they turned the task over to specialists.

Undeniably careers and careerism had a alternate meaning for the Sixties generation than was the case of the Abstract Expressionists who, by comparison, were oafish bohemians in their public dealings. Museums, too, were prompted to retain high-powered professional fund-raisers, grant writers, and image-makers who forged a different climate for the arts than was true in the pre-war New York, and their crowded restaurants and thriving gift shops have spilled out beyond the museums' walls, not to mention their well-stocked bookstores, expensive catalogues and publications, concerts, lecture series, and their other "high profile" and income-producing activities. One might even want to recall that at the beginning of the 1960s, there were almost no museum entrance fees.

The apparatus of the New York art world, the stirring up of public careers, and the promotion of new styles and movements that ensued in the post-war period reached a level of sophistication and efficiency by the 1960s that would have put Poussinists, Rubensists and Michelangelo's Medici supporters all to shame. Modern art, by which I mean the more daring, experimental, esoteric and, broadly speaking, the art that is obscure by traditional standards, reached an ever-expanding audience, socially and spiritually anxious to participate in the new cultural activities.

The marketing of art involved wider participation than ever before, presumably coinciding with the new wealth, new power and the increase in leisure. Into this mix should be added changing educational patterns. Just as the quality of high school education steadily slipped by traditional standards, almost every American family aspired to provide their children with a "higher," i.e., college, education. In terms of sheer numbers, those who attended colleges and universities and who earned B.A.'s and M.A.'s increased geometrically. Most graduates had at least a smattering of art appreciation or an introductory art survey course — the much maligned "Pyramids to Picasso" treatment — whetting their appetites for more as well as stimulating a desire in them to accept new events. This, coupled with the trend toward expanded exposure, meant that a substantial and surely the most-influential segment of society was well disposed to accept art as a something to be treasured and contemporary art as a civic duty.

A general commitment to art and specifically to the newer artistic manifestations had complex social origins. For at least fifty years there had been a breakdown in conventional religious institutions in America, especially apparent in the larger cities and outlying suburbs. In the more remote areas of the nation, populist religious sects were successfully promoted by charismatic radio and television preachers whose tax-exempt "churches" gulled millions of followers. The "born again" movement developed into a powerful force which went on to affect presidential nominations, elections and political action.

Worship of the arts became a substitute for formal religious observance especially in the urban centers. Museums metamorphosed into sacred temples — and by a stroke of luck older ones were already conveniently designed to appear as such anyway — where on Saturdays and Sundays the search for non-materialistic values could find fulfillment. Even visiting commercial art galleries had the aura of a ritualistic cleansing for the well-to-do and the initiated, especially for those from the suburbs who sought spiritual solace to remedy their deeply materialistic lives. The migration to SoHo and 57th Street has become an appropriate and uplifting weekend activity with organized, guided trips to New York City's art centers, giving rise to a mini-industry. Experts, advisors, independent dealers and art critics along with trained psychologists have attained prominence and wealth in modern society by caressing the needs of a public for whom they function like modern shamans. The institutionalization of visits to artists' studios became an increasingly common, privileged experience, and painters and sculptors have learned to skillfully explain their work to the eager half-educated. In this context, the artists of the 1960's—1980's generation are far more articulate and skillful self-promoters than were their counterparts in an earlier time.

The sheer number of amateurs who have taken up art represent another situation that has helped spur interest in the fine arts. The "fill in the numbers" sets, which had a vogue coinciding with the 1960—1980s and became ingenious "high" art spoofs, probably rest on the lowest rung of the ladder. Devotees of these coloring book puzzles of famous paintings are aficionados at a slightly higher degree of challenge than those of children, house-bound wives and Sunday painters, as well as the elderly who are encouraged to try their hand at the real thing. Many in these categories take studio courses at college, evening adult education programs at an art school, at a "Y" or the public library. The point is that all of these people have served to expand a constituency committed to looking at, reading about and discussing art. Consider also the sheer number of individuals who own a camera, who take photographs, coinciding with the time when photography had become increasingly recognized as a legitimate artform fetching high prices, and requiring well-heeled museums to house the works, at least a portion of them with artistic goals. At a minimum, these men and women constitute a substantial portion of a well-informed and eager public prepared to accept the art explosion and who take the activity seriously as they have refined their sensibilities toward basic pictorial issues.

A meaningful share in the process of expanding awareness and positive disposition toward art on the part of a wide American public belongs to the galleries big and small, in major centers like New York and Los Angeles, but also located in small cities and towns throughout the nation. These galleries sell not only expensive, museum-quality objects from the past and the present but inexpensive paintings by unknowns, or local artists. Original affordable prints form a thriving aspect of the art business. Dealers in the main centers attract clients from everywhere. All in all and in varying degrees, they have participated in the formation of an environment favorably disposed to art in general and to modern and contemporary art in particular. The operation, for the Sixties, Seventies and Eighties, also had a powerful investment component in which a constant influx of new names and new styles was a routine requirement and where purchases were even executed by telephone; a client might order a painting of a given size, from a particular year or two by a specific artist, without even seeing a photograph of the object, much less the original.

Undeniably New York served as the mecca of art both nationally and internationally, although challenges are constant. By the late 1970's and increasingly so in the 1980s, we can observe a shift from New York, or at least a sharing of avant-garde art activity with Los Angeles and European centers, especially in Germany and Italy. Not only have costly and influential exhibitions been organized in Europe that were subsequently transported to the United States, but more significantly, European artists have become towering presences in the American art complex. This condition heralds a change in the landscape of the international art market. Contemporary German and Italian art has become a prized import in New York galleries and museums and in the rest of the country. Analogies may be drawn between the expanded importation of Beamers and Benzers or Italian design products like jewelry, high fashion clothes, shoes, furniture and refined foods. *Arte povera* is a sign of wealth, like pastasciutta, in an appropriately dadaistic perversion where the commonplace has evolved into the chic or the prized.

The flow between Europe and America, which exposed a shift from the importation of the pre-war years to the exportation of the decades immediately afterwards, is now more aptly defined as a two-way autobahn. Perhaps we will see in the next decades another change in the balance, tilted toward Europe (and even Japan, which undoubtedly represents an entirely different cultural situation). By the early 1980s, the general trade situation has seen the United States move from generating a monstrous trade surplus to crushing deficits; a parallel situation is a-building for the arts. Will the art market follow the other markets? The implication that artistic dominance moves in tandem with political and economic power may be hasty, based only on incomplete evidence. Yet the suspicion remains. As Western

European economies have begun to flourish, to an extent at the expense of America's, these same countries appear to be producing world-class artists and art movements.

Coincidence?

We should consider those explosive decades in the 1940's and 1950's as related to the United States' world position. The decade or more in which Action Painting/Abstract Expressionism overwhelmed the world scene corresponds to the acme of American financial and military might. These conditions serve as a prelude to the major issues considered here, although some of the leading artists have continued to be active. Their successors, whose first independent statements occurred at the end of the 1950s, are the focus. Approximately one third of a century, a proper definition of a generation, might be thought of as the Post-Abstract Expressionist Period or, more positively, the Pop-Op-Minimalist Generation.

Instead of offering a survey of the styles and movements for the years from about 1960 to about 1990, the currents and the trends, biographical snippets of the major figures, the interactions of one artist or movement with another, I prefer to examine the physical and social reality out of which the particular mode (or modes?) of perception arose. Furthermore, this reality is cardinal not only for the formation of art but for its understanding — a notion that may seem obvious but one that is stated all too infrequently. Only within this procedure, it is suggested, may we gain a pervasive overview, and with it, insights into meaning. With this goal in mind, we need to undertake a careful inspection of the physical environment in which art was produced, displayed and sold. The characteristic conditions found in society, especially those attached to habits of consumption, as well as conditions of perception that are intimately and inseparably related to it is the point of departure. I will also take into account issues surrounding food, from advertising it, consuming it, and treating the results. This is the most fertile area in modern society for gaining an understanding of art that it has produced.

Chapter II.
The Environment

To plot the American landscape out of which the volcano of modern art erupted after World War II and, in a basically more tame version and with a slightly alternate chronology, in Europe, we must look to the great cities and specifically New York. Most of the art that has achieved authority in America was created by artists who either centered their activity or at least maintained a toehold in New York. True, many escaped Metropolis for studios in the Hamptons, Ulster County, Northern Connecticut, Taos, or wherever; but if a single generalization might be postulated about the production of art in the second half of the twentieth century, it is that modern art is in essence an urban expression. Gone for a time are the days of painting in and from nature, the careful description of rural or exotic surroundings with inevitably nostalgic overtones, of atmosphere and sunlight, of mist and rain, of mountains and meadows. Even when studios are located in a rural setting, in restored barns, redesigned Victorian carriage houses, reconditioned garages, or cinderblock warehouses, the underlying subject retains a fundamentally urban cast. The use of studio models was abandoned long ago in favor of photographs. The aggressive, demanding, sophisticatedly plotted outpouring of art that has dominated the galleries, international biennials and museums during the past generation or more cannot be separated from the vertical city. The single factor that separates New York (and Chicago, for that matter) from Los Angeles or

Houston, where one cannot walk and encounter, is sociability, certainly on a visual level. There is a constant flow of people and people services, although in the final analysis New York remains classically and supremely antisocial.

Out of pure necessity, artists have been creatively enterprising by locating in inexpensive housing in transitional neighborhoods within New York City that inevitably become "chic" in a notably brief period of time. Think of SoHo, the East Village, Brooklyn Heights, Green Point, the Bowery (which, however, is yet to have its new day), and Long Island City. Precisely because of the artists, these neighborhoods became desirable; the artists managed, by the aura of their presence alone to gentrify run-down warehouse districts and decaying tenement quarters. Astute real estate operators might be wise to plot the migration of painters and sculptors as they arrive from all over the country and abroad to New York City and who, despite the usually prohibitive costs and the scarcity of affordable studio space, manage to unearth a neighborhood where they can live and work. After all, the Hamptons were an invention of artists who liked the nature there but also the low prices in the area just a generation ago; Greenwich Village, Santa Fe and Woodstock have had similar pasts.

Artists, and here one should include representatives of all the arts, seem to exert a positive, beneficial influence on their surroundings. To the wider community they constitute a subgroup analogous to a society of priests or witch doctors who are perceived as purifying the groves where they gather through the sheer power of their collective presence. The expectation is that in a culture where material values have taken hold like a bear trap upon every aspect of public life, the need for such individuals is especially pressing. Alternatives are nonexistent. The political leadership has become incurably cynical, especially in light of the enormity of the problems that the nation and the city face. Roads and bridges are disintegrating, transportation systems are worse than they were a half century before, the cities are inundated by garbage, the air saturated with infection, cancer rates soar, AIDS is an awful reality that threatens to choke resources, drugs are gnawing away at the future. Racial tensions, which have spread to Europe's leading cities, may never have been higher. Religious leaders, virtual anachronisms, have become powerless or lack the necessary commitment or resolve, while educators have all but abandoned the eventuality of engaging their students to face spiritual or moral issues. Modern society turns, I suspect, to creative artists, all free-lancers, as the rear guard, the final hope for salvation from ruin, corruption and greed. And if this scenario contains even a grain of truth, the burden that society has heaped upon its artists is overpowering and not without risks. What happens when the actual or presumed conservators of moral rectitude join the orgy or at least give up the fight and watch on the sidelines? Such a dreadful thought requires serious consideration as we continue our attempt to understand the art produced by the generation of the 1960s—1980s.

The Modern City

The notion that modern art (I am referring to its more contemporary manifestations), as with practically every movement and style in the

Western tradition, has inseparable ties with the society from which it is produced, is a blatantly self-evident and possibly simplistic notion. Indeed, modern art is the life and culture of the society. Even in the more conservative, that is to say attributional or iconographic methodologies practiced by historians of art, to treat the Florentine Renaissance of Masaccio, Uccello, and Donatello, without reference to Cosimo de' Medici, the merchant society, and the intellectual interests of the Humanists, is quite unthinkable. The contributions of Courbet, Manet and the Impressionists, especially recently, have been studied within an economic and social context, rather than as an isolated and rarefied aesthetic happening.

Strictly speaking, however, the art of the past 30 years has rarely been contemplated within the optic of its environment or the social conditions that define its moment. Yet, is it really possible to maintain that JFK or Richard Nixon, the Eisenhower Years, the Reagan policies, had nothing whatsoever to do with the art that was produced during these regimes? However, a near total lack of interest in exploring conditions outside of art itself by the critical apparatus devoted to contemporary art is the rule rather than the exception. Presumably unpleasant or non-aesthetic elements make critics uncomfortable, they prefer instead more antiseptic factors, issues of style or the presumed constant meaningful traditions linking past and present art. They tend to advocate an interpretation in which forms or solutions that on the surface appear quite unique relate to esoteric events in past art rather than facing underlying political, social, economic and environmental events. To correct this misunderstanding is a desideratum of this study.

At the risk of sounding obvious, I maintain that contextual conditions unavoidably regulate the thinking of artists, permitting or actually prompting their expression, and have also inescapably oriented the public that looks and buys the art. Only if we retrace the conditions in which the art was created can we hope to gain insights into the meaning of the total phenomenon. The single individual contributions of the artists also must be approached similarly. A more ambitious objective requires a larger scope beyond and behind the arts if one seeks enlightenment with the aspiration of improving the situation, naturally presupposing that the situation could benefit from adjustments.

An assumption that derives from any superficial exploration of contemporary urban life is that the two-dimensional image continues as a pervasive, engaging and even hypnotic format, indispensable for modern communication and expression. Images, that is, pictorial events involving illusionism on a flat surface exercise a constant, pervasive, and inescapable power over the daily lives of the entire society, holding a fascination that has, if anything, increased in recent generations. The ready accessibility of pictorial imagery, and especially its familiarity as insistently experienced, has seduced the public into believing that they comprehend the medium. Even when painting is rendered in rigorously space-denying configurations, where three-dimensionalizing devices are for all practical purposes effectively eliminated: linear perspective, overlapping planes or forms, alternating sizes, and modeling to create volume, the implications of illusionism nonetheless are unavoidable. As artists have sought to emphasize the flatness of the picture plane, the purely two-dimensional quality of painting as, say, in a collage when one color area is juxtaposed with another, including the extreme case of a single color occupying a painting's entire field, spatial events inevitably enter. Even when a canvas is tinged with one evenly applied tone, as a white surface, vibrations that imply another dimension are set into motion; it seems to be unavoidable, impossible to cancel.

The intensity of experiencing pictorial figuration emanating from the mass media must be taken into account. Consider also the ever-present printed word in newspapers and magazines. Reading a book or article where the letters and words are spread out in even rows on a flat surface, on a page or on a computer screen, are constant visual as well as mechanical encounters. We are oriented to approaching images as we do words — two-dimensionally — since we are being constantly bombarded by them, so that when confronted with a painting, a print, or a photograph, our response system finds familiar and consoling turf.

This common two-dimensionalized habit of perception finds constant confirmation in the urban environment. I have selected an area running alongside the campus of a world-class but declining university on the longest and broadest of the New York avenues where an uninterrupted confrontation with the central city may be obtained. The mental orientation of city dwellers, the pattern of their reflexes are observed and, more relevant to the theme of this book, the signification of the objects, that is, the sculptures and especially the paintings that artists living in New York produce, may be illustrated in context. A person's behavior is, in large measure, determined by their physical surroundings. How much more vivid are the responses of fine artists to the same visual stimuli? The regular, customary and routine contact with the world which we encounter obviously affects our moods, behavior, perception and mode of visualization. We rapidly begin to "look like" and "act like" our environment: husbands and wives, after decades of marriage, accumulate each other's characteristics, and even our domestic pets absorb the natures of their masters. In shifting the anthropomorphic bias, I cannot imagine that we fail entirely to take on the personality characteristics of our pets, as part of an exchange. I believe that the city has a determining effect upon its dwellers and what they produce, an essential assumption for what follows.

Artists in the City

When we examine American contemporary art and the contribution of diverse artists, strict categorization according to presumed social class has no apparent value. Class patterns are virtually impossible to decipher since practicing artists come from all social levels and ethnic groups, with probably the greatest number from that broad unspecific and indefinable "middle class," to which most Americans think they belong anyway, however rich or poor they happen to be. Even in the 1930s when there was a good deal more class consciousness, efforts to politically organize artists proved to be relatively hopeless. More to the point is the fact that artists constitute a social class of their own merely by the fact of being artists. Standing on the edge of formal structures, they have access to the entire society, while being at once slightly outside the border.

Since World War II most painters and sculptors who in previous generations trained in art schools and academies have endured a certain amount of college education, frequently majoring in art or in one of the humanistic disciplines. On the whole, then, fine artists have shared an educational pattern with their patrons, dealers, jurors of grant-giving foundations, not to mention their spokespersons and critics, although in college they were often able to concentrate or major in studio programs, and already were, by choice, somewhat set apart from the main body of students. This type of training and experience in the ivy halls of colleges and universities provides a distinctive orientation separate from that found in "pure" art schools. The surroundings where education unfolded with powerful cultural paraphernalia permitted exchanges that reflected a departure from the norms of the past. Many practicing artists today hold MFA degrees which provide a diploma permitting them to teach but which also serve as evidence of formal programmed training. In particular, artists of the generation of the 1960s–1980s are, on the whole, remarkably literate and often effectively verbal. They are skilled at expressing themselves in words as well as with colors, in contrast to their counterparts from previous generations, and consequently are better able to conduct a public career.

Recent art is both popularist and urban. Furthermore, in the past half century life in the city has undergone intense changes of its own. The city, and here I refer specifically to New York but by analogy other cities, welcomes artists, but it also modifies and organizes their modes of thinking and, still more to the point, of seeing. On the other side of the coin, of course, the modern city is itself changed by the presence of artists in consistent numbers who reside there, a condition that further emphasizes the requirement of turning to the physical city in a search for insights into the manifestations of art.

Criticism of contemporary art that relies upon an explication of styles and "influences" and their presumed interactions reflects an approach based upon formalistic references to previous as well as contemporary manifestations, and it dominates current writing and thinking about art. The initiated will immediately find satisfaction in the assertion: "Middle Mondrian influenced Barnett Newman at a crucial stage, whose art, in turn, saw a revival in the 1980s, but with renewed impulses from late Matisse." The approach represented in this methodology offers confidence to the dedicated believer that he has the situation well in hand and under perfect control. Yet, it seems to me, the system of contemporary art criticism is structureless and thoroughly circular, offering little space for effective control. To be sure, art comment from earlier eras depended on a similar approach, one based on the identification of "sources" and "influences." Such criticism is effective only to the extent that the referents are obscure enough to bewilder all but the true cognoscenti, however. It can easily become an exclusive parlor game for professionals and the circle of persons surrounding them. Particularly insidious, the approach appears to offer enlightenment or a viable "handle" for understanding a given artist, or particular art movement, or an epoch. For the semi-educated collector or art buyer in a bank or corporation, the approach is particularly deceptive, since by actually "seeing" connections, they are easily deluded into thinking that they are in command of the situation. Besides, by unraveling complex interinfluences, the innocent might actually confuse the explanation with something like artistic quality or aesthetic brilliance. More valid modes of understanding are needed. Nothing in what I have said precludes the fact that Barnett Newman actually was taken with middle Mondrian; rather, the challenge lies in using that fact for some sort of insight into either Mondrian or Newman which, in turn, begins to explain what they were about and why. Nonetheless, I am convinced that such inquiries should not be the main weapons when attacking the difficulties of explaining art, modern or traditional.

In a related situation, when dealing with an artist and his work, the interview system has become the favored approach. The interviewer is usually a friendly critic whose task is to elicit some intelligent responses from the artist. This method is by no means limited to artists, but its widespread application does not curb the insidious nature of the process. In the first place, the format is by no means an inevitably productive one. A more serious defect is that such an interview acts as a substitute for a carefully thought-out and composed statement which not only can take the form of a finely tuned literary presentation, but can be rethought. The interview format itself, often with questions and answers, is an artificial situation in the first place, with a mechanics all of its own. Furthermore, after a few interviews, the artist may be even less prone to set down his ideas in a coherent statement, if indeed he is prone to do so, assuming that everything he has to say has already been said in the interviews.

To return to the city, a particularly splendid time is the early morning, especially during the spring or fall when nearly every aspect is sharply revealed, undeflected by the throngs, the discomfort of excessive cold or its opposite, when ninety degree temperatures and with the humidity at the same cipher awaken the unappetizing odors of rotting garbage. Of course, one is required to return during more populated hours and in all four seasons to capture the complete panorama.

The Fade In/Fade Out, Turn On/Turn Off Syndrome

Before actually examining the physical aspects of the modern city, a characteristically urban reflex pattern of behavior requires explanation, one that crops up everywhere, in Rome, Paris and London. Probably the most remarkable aspect of modern seeing, the fade in/fade out syndrome is readily detectable in its most elaborated version in New York City. Although not entirely a new phenomenon, its manifestations are most readily observed in crowded urban environments, those mysterious entities known as neighborhoods.

Extremely unsavory, really repulsive circumstances that one experiences are customarily abruptly and automatically veiled; they are faded out of vision, channeled to slide from the mind's eye into a limbo of non-existence. Like a television soap opera, the slaughter on Beijing's Tiananmen Square, children being killed regularly by stray bullets in the heart of the city, a plane crash in the Alps, can all be eliminated in a second when by merely pressing the OFF button on the remote or the delete key on the laptop. Furthermore, those unpleasant, intolerable aspects of life that are switched off achieve the same reality and, of course, the same unreality as the teleplay or devastating mass starvation report on central Africa, an earthquake in the Philippines, AIDS, hostages taken and released-occurrences perceived in an identical manner take on the character of fables. In an odd reversal of the expected, the more "real" the experience, the more horrific and depressing, the more easily it can be dissolved out of existence. The greenhouse effect or the problems connected with the ozone layer cannot be all that bad. Does sunbathing really hurt people? Did the fallout from Chernobyl really destroy hundreds of thousands of acres of rich farmland for decades and cause cancer in tens of thousands of victims? Do sacred doctors engage in tens-of-thousands of unnecessary operations annually? Do dentists drill dubious cavities galore? Click it off, who wants to know all that anyway? In terms of perception, the ease with which we can tune in and out, turn on and off, has to be regarded as one of the most remarkable aspects of contemporary life, one that is epitomized by the computer that operates by an endless series of yeses and noes. And, to continue the analogy, the computer manages to keep the deleted item in RAM for a round or two, just in case one might desire to retrieve it from the region of departed spirits.

By removing the bum who peed in his soggy, shapeless trousers, the drug addict, the alcoholic, the drunken Noah who has fallen desperately out of control on the sidewalk at our feet, from active vision, reasoning, and intelligence, he is permitted to fade into nonexistence, to a state of never having existed. By clouding over the mountains of filth stacked in shabby ill-proportioned mounds at the bowel-exits of every building, the possibility to function daily, to gather food, provide shelter, shepherd a family and other basic required tasks is preserved. See no evil...the survival of the fittest...are operative concepts. One has to be reminded of the obverse—that is, country life—calm rural settings, the woods—in other words, a relatively unperverted nature. America offers ample zones of such landscapes, even quite near the metropolitan areas, where the eye can linger on the edge of a pond, on a few rocks, on a clump of brush, an unsubstantial dandelion, without the need to tune out, to turn off. Yet, modern art is not made in such a context; probably it cannot be, at least in the configurations that have been presented to us thus far. The capacity for rapidly tuning out while staying tuned in is a habit inherited from radio where one switched stations and waves-lengths, languages, programming, kinds of music, sounds, jingles—a set of conditions well understood by John Cage. Even earlier, the electric light switch functioned quite unlike the candle or oil lamp, with no preparation required except the raising or lowering of a knob. Maybe Picasso was telling us something of this sort when he located an electric light bulb in such a central position in the Guernica, arguably the most influential painting of the 20th century.

Beginning ten or so years ago, changing from one television channel to another was facilitated by the remote control, meaning that one could switch around to one's heart's content from the comfort of the waterbed, without interrupting nibbling on cheese-flavored popcorn. Today's viewer tends to schizophrenically move from one program to another, firing his electronic gun at the screen, from one unreal, manufactured situation to another, and then back again, from drama, to twenty-two giants contesting an oddly shaped, air-filled leather object, political speeches, Easter Mass from the Vatican by satellite, cable hard, medium and soft porno, and advertising spots, in what has become a normal, habitual procedure. The percentage of viewers who actually follow two and even three programs simultaneously might be close to the majority, certainly among the younger population whose boredom tolerance is fragile, so they surf the channels frantically. Not only can one, with split screen viewing, follow two or three shows at the same time, but they can be tuned in and out at a pace that makes the entire experience a bewildering hodgepodge of images. Perfect reflections of these intensified visual splicings are the popular music videos, skillfully and even intelligently produced, at least from a technical point of view, in which the imagery changes almost from second to second. These repeated and thus common, if not "normal," experiences cannot fail to have an impact upon the perception of everything, including the art. I also suggest that these patterns affect not only our perception of the real world, but condition our fantasies and our dreams.

The on-off reaction in the streets infects new residents of the city with frightening rapidity, after even a few hours, so that they join with the inveterate city-dweller in the mode of perceiving the immediate, at-hand world. No doubt the process is set into motion by instinctive self preservation systems. Yet the apparitions, the misery regularly encountered and then clicked off, must be there anyway, lurking in the psyche, bobbing up unexpectedly in our data bank, modifying our actions, gnawing away at our consciences, and affecting our mode of comprehending the world and the art.

The fade in/fade out process has become a fundamental aspect of perception that affects how art is experienced. How often does a viewer enter a gallery or a room in a museum, make the grand sweep with the head, glancing from one work to another in a few moments, and finally utter some qualitative sweeping generalization? Conception of art cannot pretend to be immune to the same operations, and presumably the actual invention and production of the art is itself predicated on similar circumstances.

The Sidewalks

On those honorable, majestic sidewalks, wide enough to carry a full lane of automobile traffic, the typical sight at dawn includes blown wads of black and white newspapers highlighted with bits of color, loose sheets, patterned wrappings, agonized brown bags twisted at the top whose shapes still remember what they once contained: tightly clasped bottles of booze. Colored plastic sacks with lettering, logos and slogans on them, aluminum soda cans whose designed surfaces come in every hue and color, empty, often broken bottles, mostly pints or flask-like half pints that once housed sweet wine or insidious mixes of vodka or gin and sugary mints and lemon flavors whose pale greenish memories still outline the bottom of the receptacles. If it happens that it was windy, the entire area is covered with blown slippery newsprint and other refuse which one must wade through: paper plates with red-blotch memories of the pizza slice it previously hosted, transparent sheets from chocolatey brownies, Gyro wrappers, shish kebab sticks, ice cream cups and occasionally an accompanying miniature plastic spoon, potato chip sacks, cigarette butts, cardboard boxes and their inserts from the neighborhood stores. If it happened to have rained the night before, the newspapers are glued in variously shaped undulating lumps to the surface, hardening as they dry like a miniature relief map of the Sahara.

The appearance of the sidewalks is a revealing yet mystifying feature of the area, especially within the context of contemporary art. As a continuous plane, like a vast unraveled carpet, mosaic, or endless airport painting, with activated zones subdivided into noble squares or rectangles of diverse sizes and proportions, all retain a close rapport to human scale. More pertinently, the sections are in measurement analogous to familiar units conventionally found in the fine art galleries. Each section may be comprehended independently, isolated by a "frame", articulated by grooves, or viewed as an infinite series pertaining either to an entire side of the square city block, or as a still larger unit comprising all four sides of the block, or an essentially unending world cycle encompassing the entire city. Undoubtedly, we are well-prepared to experience the sidewalk under the tutelage of modern developments in art.

The surface of the walkway is never quite level, sloping this way or that even within the more restricted units and has general propensities, sometimes inclining upward or down for the entire block or a series of blocks only to turn back the other way. One or another of the smallest units may appear level, or a few of them together may; but, like the earth, we know better.

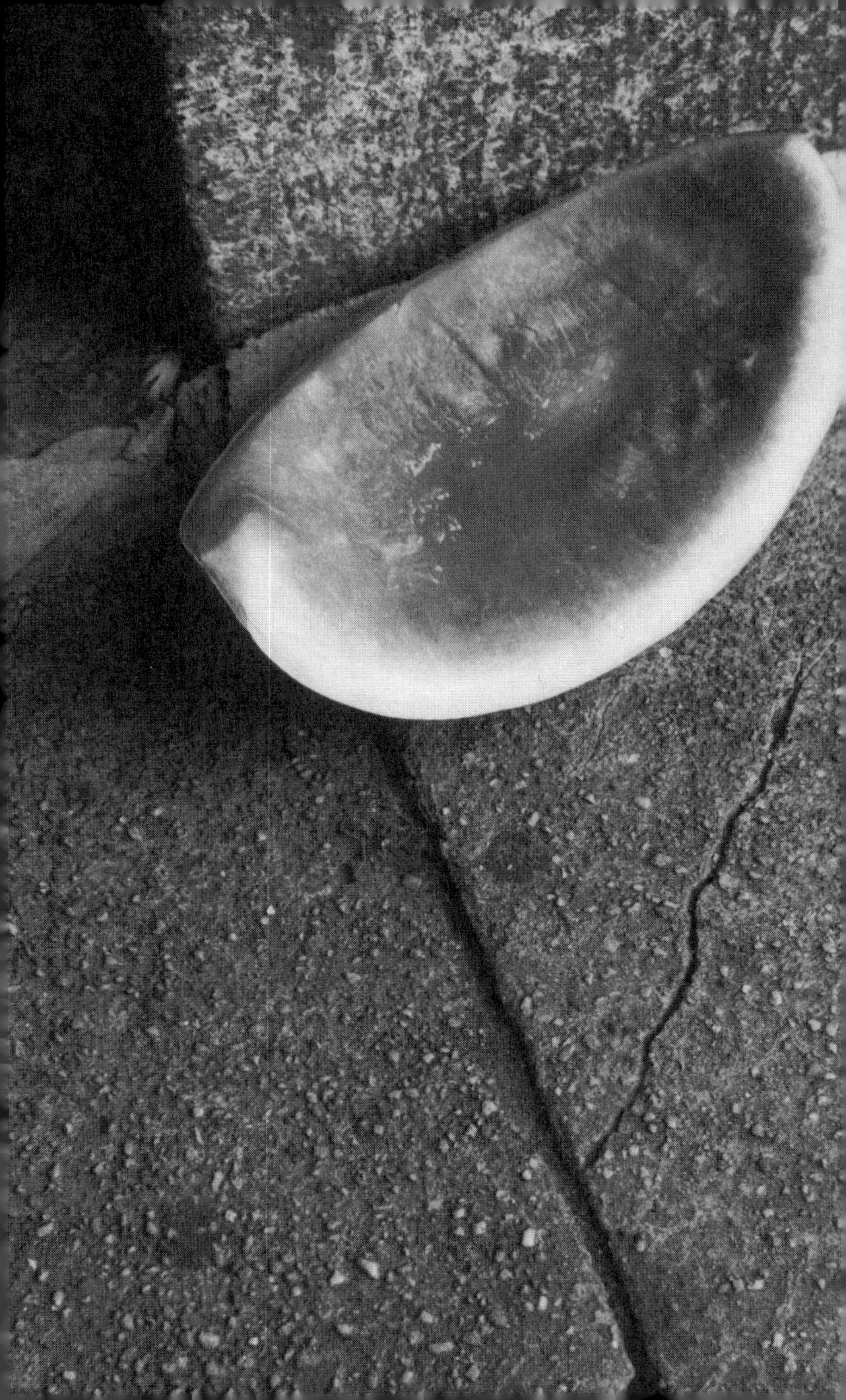

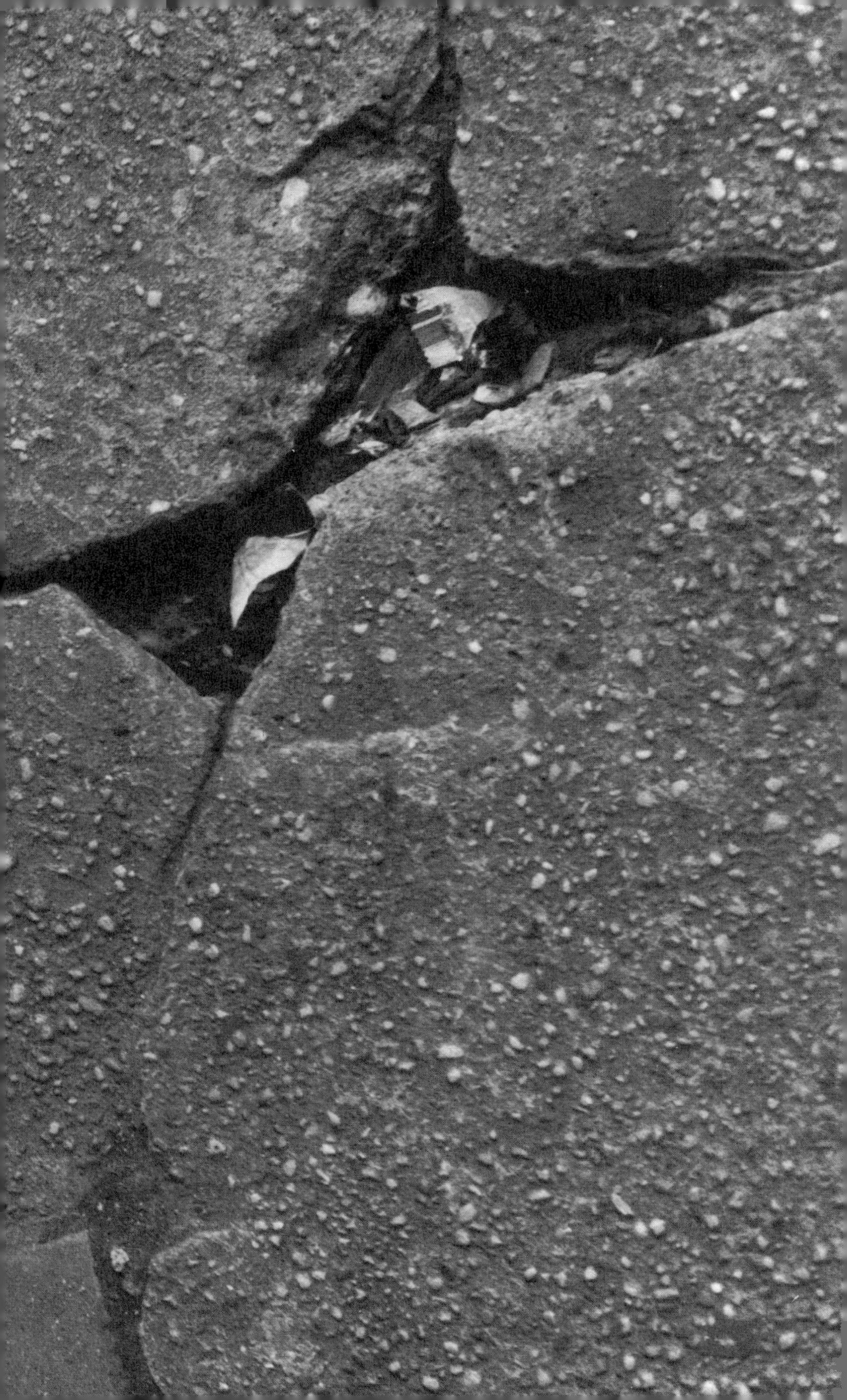

Neither is the surface uniform: sometimes it is granular, similar to the heavy weaves of 16th and 17th century canvases, tapestries, or the even more nubby surfaces of burlap, favored from time to time by recent artists. In the cases where the surfaces are fairly smooth, connections may be drawn with finely woven duck canvas, or murals, or even panel paintings on prepared wood. Notwithstanding the internal diversity, the surface may be understood as a familiar carrier of two-dimensional imagery, as evidenced by sidewalk painters who, with colored chalk, brighten the walkways with recollections of Michelangelo's pre-restored Sistine Ceiling, until washed away by iconoclasts or simply by a warm summer rain.

The sidewalks are cracked and spliced, split and crushed: gaping holes have been drilled into them to make room for hydrants; poles and meters have been injected into their sides, their skins have been trimmed, shaved or they have merely succumbed to old age, full of lines and crevices. Moss and grass grow in them following predetermined patterns to create green monotypes laid upon pale tones. Words, names, slogans and infantile prehistoric designs are inscribed in, on or over them. Inevitably, foreign substances have been attached. They are pissed on by man and beast, crapped on, vomited on, eaten on, wept on, stumbled on, fallen on, slept on, swept on and possibly, though rarely, screwed on. They have been splashed and dripped on, they have been painted and toned. Cafes rest on them and awnings shield them from sun, rain and bird droppings. Life situations can be reconstructed from shadowy stains on them like the Holy Shroud of Turin. The sidewalk is the most common, virtually continuous visual experience for the city dweller, where a living theater unfolds daily with the spectator/observer functioning as a basic contributor and lead actor in the formulation of the presentation.

Sidewalk slabs are by no means all the same color; they reflect the material from which they are composed, varying from a warm light-toned tan obtained as if with a touch of burnt sienna, to a creamy white, to a cooler bluish gray and tones in between. Their appearance, like blank screens, also is determined in part by the light and the colors that surround them: neon pizza signs, the sky, flashing police cars and ambulances. Sometimes, miniaturized mica mirrors flicker on and off in the sunlight, producing a magical silvery effect.

In New York these days, the sidewalks are laid down piecemeal, following the outlines of century-old originals while taking some liberties. As the need arises for renovations or repairs (gas, electric, sewage, and water lines), the sidewalks are smashed with jackhammers. Then, for weeks or even months, pale, freshly dug earth with stones and rocks just like those found outside the city, is irregularly piled up on either side of the gaping openings with traffic barriers and luminescent orange and white plastic tape sloppily attached to anything convenient as a signal for people to stand clear. After a few days, garbage inevitably gets tossed in: soda cans, empty bottles, plastic containers and miscellaneous debris are rammed into the piles of dirt, all of which eventually gets dumped back into the hole and sealed until the next round. A new section of sidewalk is poured. Here and there, as the need arises, alterations of this kind have occur over the decades at an unplanned and aimless pace, forming irregular configurations.

After the viscous concrete is freshly laid, the temptation is irresistible to scribble a word or image, or one's initials, with a stick or forefinger. A doodle, freezing into the sidewalk for posterity one's private mark, a low relief graffito, sometimes partially obliterated by a frustrated but conscientious mason before final setting. Perhaps the most noticeable aspect of such inscriptions is the absence of political messages, which is also true of the graffiti on the base of buildings, on boards, busses and subway cars and platforms around the city. The messages are inevitably personal either proclaiming one's existence, affections, or the virtues of a girlfriend: graffito seems to be an exclusively male mode of expression (though I am not absolutely sure of the assertion).

Most people are neither conscious nor terribly concerned with the sidewalk except when it is broken or when they are attentively avoiding some creature or tripping over unexpected obstacles. Nevertheless, the sidewalk is a compelling constant backdrop for an array of visual and optical stimuli: a continuous presence for the city dweller, like the sky, irrepressibly modifying vision, sometimes at the front plane of consciousness, but frequently in more subliminal terrain, a sonorous backdrop for actions, sights and sounds. Here we encounter friends, as on the *piazze* of other times and other places, and shy away from enemies, frantically clicking off eye contact when encountering the hapless and the homeless, the druggies and desperate, aggressive teenagers, the crazies.

At distinct corners, standing at crooked attention near where the sidewalks have been shaved and ribbed to facilitate the handicapped's transition from sidewalk to street, are battered wire trash cans crammed full of refuse, forming images that participate in the wasteland as fixed landmarks, sentinels guarding the crossways. Such an unsightly, unhealthy, and damaging specter is blanked from awareness by the automatic control switches, repressed only if one fights with furious determination to hold onto the sight. Yet systematically reading these trash cans hardly appeals to many people anyway, so we just click them away.

After we are exposed to the still-life elements, the posts, the hydrants, the columns of pipe, human drama begins to take center stage. Panhandlers (an outmoded word because nowadays they use tattered, filthy and impermanent plastic coffee cups and not metal pans for handouts), bums or, more in line with contemporary jargon and fact, the homeless are only momentarily shocking. Beginning in early morning, these shabby Dantean shades begin to filter onto that broad way, stretching in the doorways and in other vaguely protected coves offered by the modern city. Those who rise at dawn or who have never slept are preparing for the daily scavenge for food and drink: to finance breakfast, for the first swig of wine or sweetened liquor, for a fix. Usually with personally tailored, ingenious approaches, or "hooks," as skillfully devised as any invented by Madison Avenue advertising execs, the day begins. The line may consist of a catchy opener, a pitiful and practiced look of calculated misery that is probably a survival technique of historic antiquity passed into the vocabulary of daily use by vagabonds and urban nomads; or the stylized manner of dress in found rags, whimsically arranged in creative combinations, either for the purpose of attention

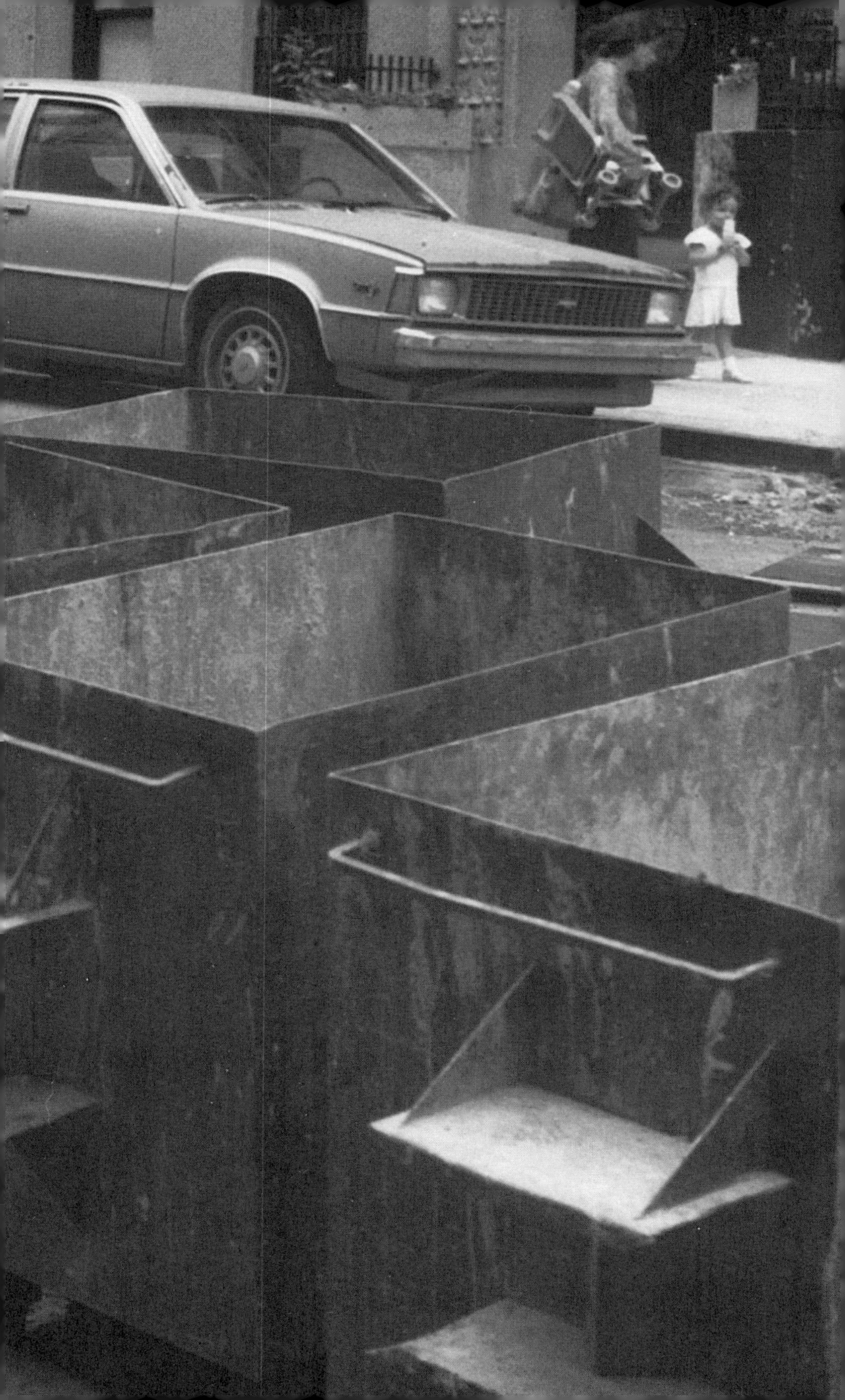

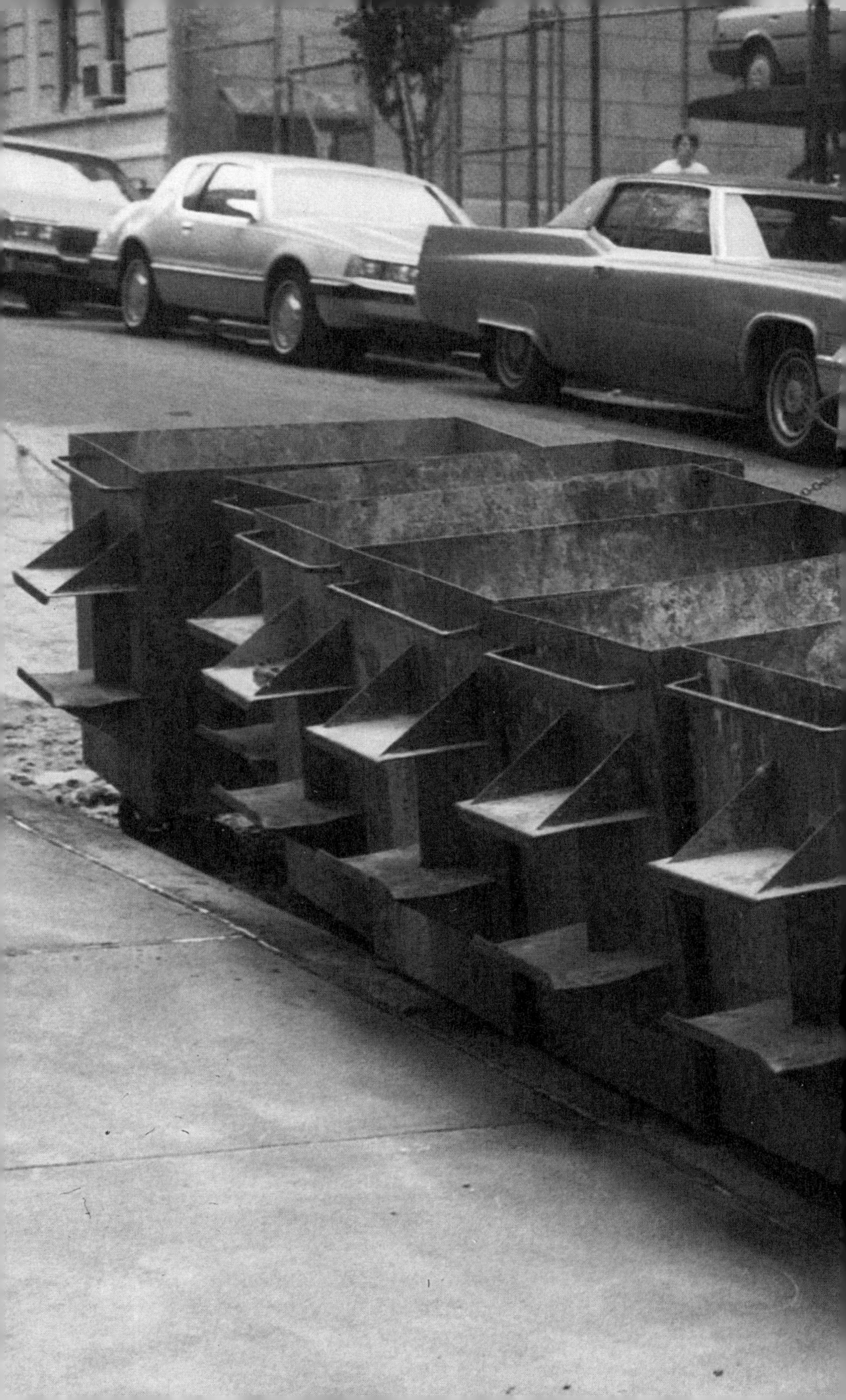

getting or as a means of broadcasting their own individuality. Once the bait has been nibbled, total refusal by an early-morning passersby rushing off to work is impossible, especially since a one-to-one rapport is more difficult to avoid when there are few people on the street. "Avoid eye contact if you want to be left alone," we are advised: fade out, and turn up the volume on the Walkman. *Lucy In the Sky With Diamonds.*

The mounds of refuse are specifically nauseating for the novice observer but are hardly even noticed by the veteran urbanite; one matures quickly in the city, fading out, clicking off. Yet the *merde* remains there, somewhere in the crevices of the brain, forming a festering component, probably an intrinsic one, in the visual environment and in the habits of perception. How could it be otherwise?

In conjunction with these physical stimuli, unseen factors are also ever-present ones, usually left to the arena of rhetoric: questions of air pollution, sound pollution, acid rain falling on the lakes and seas, destruction of the ozone layer, the poisons we ingest in unspecified quantities daily merely by breathing, the endless medications and drugs. The effect upon contemporary life of the regular, inescapable, all-embracing bombardment of street experiences has to be enormous, even if there are no documented studies with telltale numbers, bar graphs and computer-generated charts, boring away at the foundations of our being.

Physical surroundings in all their aspects have a decisive effect on the art produced, observed, judged and even purchased by persons immersed in the same surroundings. The entire edifice must be understood as determining contemporary creation in the arts. Although such a proposition may appear obvious, it remains remote, has been tuned out, turned off with the same mechanisms as individual, unpleasant encounters are turned off with a mere click of the switch.

The body politic appears to be able to switch on or off moral and ethical issues with the same ease. Everyone is appalled by what they confront on those blocks; most feel sorry for the pathetic individuals they confront and willingly enough dip into their pockets for spare change, only to immediately switch channels. These terrible scenes disappear, at least for a stretch of street or a piece of time, only to be turned on again as we hunt for the all-sports or all-news, all-financial, all-sex or all-weather channel.

The Cars

New York City sidewalks and people do not make an exclusive claim on our attention. On the wide avenue with a green median strip down the center and beside the curbs of the side streets that intersect it, automobiles of every size, tiny outdated Renault Fives and decrepit VW Bugs, along with an homogeneous array of Japanese imports, are randomly interspersed with home-spawned models. A common denominator shared with the universally poor design and unfulfilling color of all of them is that democratically and without prejudice they are prey to break-ins. We often see, on any given early morning, broken shards of shatter-proof glass scattered on the street and encroaching onto the sidewalk from crushed side windows, as if they were caught in the process of regressing to the original state from which they were produced. In the night, usually towards dawn, he chooses a single side of entire blocks, but rarely both sides, in search of money, drugs, decent clothes, salable radios and tape decks, as well as miscellanies that might have been left behind on the back seats. Although, of course, the ultimate theft, the final solution, is the car itself.

Even those experienced city folk who, with sage cynicism, have taken time out to print in legible block letters, in wobbly crayon strokes or flow pens, signs reading "NO DRUGS, NO RADIO, NO NOTHING" or "RADIO ALREADY STOLEN," sometimes written bilingually in Spanish and English, are not automatically immune to the crowbar, the favored instrument employed in smashing sprees. The event is so common that commercially preprinted signs are available with a choice of texts at well-equipped hardware stores around the city, obviously supplying a consistent demand. A small number of brave souls leave their cars unlocked on purpose, hoping to save the cost and nuisance of repairing a smashed window, but they run the unsavory risk that their cars become a crash pad for the night, a place to shoot up, the location of a one-night-stand, or worse, a private toilet.

Window breaking has become a norm, a way of life, an egalitarian leveler where everyone, rich and poor, professor and student, woman and man, black or white, gay or straight, is treated as an equal, although the well-heeled have solved the problem by paying for a garage whose monthly rates are roughly equivalent to the rent of a decent studio apartment up–state. In contrast to a couple of decades ago, the overnight parking problem on the Upper West Side has vanished: now the question has become whether you will find your car the next morning and in what condition.

On a positive note, from the point of view of providing jobs and moving money around, the auto glass replacement industry thrives. Anxious lines of angry but resigned owners queue up an hour or two before the 8 a.m. opening to be assured that their precious machines will be whole again by the end of the working day. Or they make their own temporary repairs with silver duct tape and brown cardboard or transparent plastic that at least keeps the wind and cold out. In this wounded state the cars are even more vulnerable prey, though experienced thieves realize that there is nothing left to take. The sensation of having been violated is coupled with an awful recognition that there has been a total breakdown of law and order; together they provoke disgust, depression and helplessness on the part of the victims. The authorities admit they are powerless to deal with this plague of petty crime that usually produces damage to the innocent public to the tune of hundreds of dollars a shot, depending on the rarity of the model. Anyway, owning a car has a very different meaning for a city dweller than for someone in the suburbs or the country, since in most cases a car is a luxury, considering among other things the infinitely high insurance rates and special taxes. Yet the automobile represents a safety valve permitting weekend escapes and the avoidance of the degrading, inefficient and even dangerous mass transportation system.

The random combination of industrial colors of the autos, as they strike an observer, requires a comment within any visual analysis of the urban environment: those maroons, popular some years ago, the metallic silvers and blues, or the cult of metalized heavy grays more recently in vogue. Each has a sociology, but all of them are at best unrelated to nature, and together they constitute an unrewarding, ever-present backdrop to city life.

Beyond the programmed artificiality of colors surely based on expensive consumer surveys and public testing, another prevalent aspect of the scene is that a substantial number, probably most, of the cars that regularly sit on the public streets have been bumped, battered, scratched, crunched or dented, with broken back lights and bent fenders, consequently on display in various states of abuse and decay. Once bashed, and if not cured at a bodyshop hospital, the car's wounds fester rapidly from rust, pollution and vandalism. The array of vehicles, some parked tight to the curb, others a foot or more away, a few properly parallel, the remainder with noses or rear ends sticking out, already has the disorderly logic of a junk yard. This apparition is another of those sights the urbanite easily tunes out, hardly recognizing that it exists, although without anything like a clear mind one arrives at the distinct impression that the parked cars are on the straight and narrow path until their Last Judgment: demolition — as the natural consequence of poor design, bad luck, and human and environmental hazards.

Among more or less junky autos parked on the curb-sides, a surrealistic twist of the deteriorating norm stands out from time to time: the car of an aficionado, not necessarily a Puerto Rican apartment house superintendent in the neighborhood but usually one, proudly shining his low mileage, impeccably cared-for sky-blue Impala. Then, inevitably and to the disgrace of the entire community and perhaps the entire world, one dreadful day when the scales of justice have gone amok, the much-loved and indulged 10 year old car is bashed by a truck or stolen by a couple of kids for a joy ride.

Sometimes, cars on the street are raided by predators with a conscience, limiting their attacks to those machines parked on the same spot for a period of days or weeks or that have accumulated a set of parking tickets. For the experienced eye the meaning is clear: these cars had been stolen and abandoned after the gasoline in the tank had been consumed. Such cars, including the 1978 blue Chevy, are raided in stages by a sequence of specialists: first, those who take the wheels, presumably for the tires. For a reason that escapes me, they place the cars on makeshift blocks, like stolen milk crates, so as not to rest the wheelless axles directly on the payment. Probably the custom derives from the need to prevent accidents as the thieves remove the wheels one by one and is not really a courtesy. Those who strip the engines of salable parts usually arrive next, opening the hoods by force or more simply releasing the latches from the inside. Batteries are in demand but also generator/alternators and other semi-independent transplantable organs, parts that must be maintained in an active computerized second-hand market with national retrieval. The buyers are mainly smaller repair shops and garages who palm off the stolen parts as new factory originals to their unsuspecting customers or do-it-yourselfers anxious to save cash, in the illicit but lucrative recycling process.

De rigueur, trunks are jimmied open early in the dissection process. The metal plate added to the trunk for increased protection, inexcusably required simply because the standard equipment locks are so easily bypassed, is only a minor obstacle. The hope eternal is that behind the protective plate one will find a hidden cache: guns, a junkie's supply of drugs or better yet a dealer's stash. Doctors' cars are particularly sought after. Even if there is nothing of value, a spare tire, either those insulting miniature ones sold with new cars or old-fashioned, worn spares hardly worth more than a couple of bucks. Poor consolation, but everything helps, including the jack that served to remove the wheels.

The bloodless corpses, hoods and trunk doors gaping open, limbs amputated and inner parts removed for eventual transplants, rest on their death beds for weeks. Then, usually before a random burning, a city tow truck miraculously turns up as if by sheer chance at an unlikely hour to carry the carcass off to an auto graveyard. The hallucinatory appearance of cars on the city streets forms a basic, embracing visual circumstance of city life, providing a constant stage set, much like the sidewalks that they abut.

The cars' diverse shapes, sizes, colors and forms in varying states of decomposition, provide an ever-present, semi-permanent visual experience whenever we travel by foot, bus, automobile or in a typically rickety yellow cab. Taxis could furnish an entire chapter of a book on New York, especially the drivers, with their varied origins, exotic languages, previous occupations, two-family houses in Queens and laconic philosophical slant on life in the city. The cabs' interiors are worthy of precise systematic description, beginning with moralistic "No Smoking" signs, either ready-mades or handwritten, oval photographs of children and, when appropriate, grandchildren, little altars with sacred statuettes enlivened by tiny plastic flowers. They contain translucent separators intended to protect vulnerable drivers from robbers or worse that are punctured by a little two-way ash tray for passing the money, while makeshift repairs usually with ubiquitous silver duct tape that after a time blackens with dirt around the stringy edges and begins to peel, are constantly noticeable. These machines are kept alive by constant improvisation, managing to carry a heavy load of inner city travelers in their battered hulks. They are a significant constant yellow stream in the urban landscape, representing a haven, an emblem of salvation, during personal emergencies and heavy rains; on those occasions they are happily switched on. A refinement of the usual cab is the gypsy which is merely a modified regular car, sometimes quite elegantly attired, whose status is at best semi-legal, and probably not insured.

Cars, taxis, buses, garbage scows, and monstrous Mac trucks moving at different speeds create flashes of color, in varying sizes, magnitudes, and fluctuating intensities. Although sound is not considered here, one cannot entirely disregard the high decibel level and variety of noises that issue from below ground and from the street, from the blaring ghetto blaster held by a pathetic adolescent or from cruising cars with Rock and Roll bouncing from building to building, to refuse haulers grinding their sustenance with horrible indigestion. Into this cacophony of conflicting sounds, the faint strains of Mozart may be heard thinly from the headset of a trim middle-aged jogger. The bystander who may be stationary or moving at a walking pace is confronted with flights of color flashing past like animals in the jungle, sometimes headed in the same direction as he is but at different speeds or in the opposite direction, participating in a intricate visual pattern that inevitably impacts upon his mode of perception. The coloristic backdrop on the stage in which one walks, then, has as the foreground parked autos, while in the more distant plane in the middle ground are the waves of movement irregularly interrupted by traffic lights, then on the move again in endless streams. Still further in the distance is another plane composed of an additional row of parked cars, shadowy reflections of those in the near distance.

The Dumpster

A prominent semi-monument of daily urban life is the dumpster. One of these jumbo monsters has been sitting halfway up the street from the corner of the main intersection for three years having metamorphosed into a fixed feature of the physical landscape. A construction company deposited the vast container which was transformed into a depository for every imaginable object, although its primary function is to carry off the rubble from the renovation of a nearby building. Little name plates with lettering and numbers have been applied to the thick green painted metal hide of the container, including the empty warning: DO NOT PLAY IN OR AROUND THIS HAULER, written in unreadable letters at a height no child could reach even if he stood on the shoulders of two others. The contents on any given day in any given week might include live garbage packaged in familiarly pernicious, shiny black plastic sacks or permeable, leaking bags; broken furniture, along with the appropriate rubble: ripped plaster walls and encrusted, nail-filled two-by-fours. The excrement of man's best friend, flung high up there by law-abiding pet owners, and taking on a rainbow of pale pastel shades whose origins are traceable to dog snacks and fake bones, is packaged in self-sealing transparent Baggies. Among the few noticeable quality-of-life improvements within the past decade or so is the relative disappearance from streets and parks of the dog shit that once caused New Yorkers considerable discomfort. New York seems to have it over sister cities in Europe where pampered beasts remain encouraged to leave their independent marks on the cobblestone walkways, as we find in Rome and Florence, resulting in smelly havoc for the Ferragamos and Guccis; or the menacingly huge heaps of turd deposited here and there by muscular, overfed mastiffs in Düsseldorf.

A surge of glory spotlights the dumpster once each year when the dormitory of the woman's college across the street empties out for summer vacation. The young inhabitants, one quarter of whom possess hard-earned diplomas, have vacated their cramped, dismal quarters after two arduous semesters, never to return. They discard whatever is deemed unworthy of the return trip home to one or another of America's affluent suburbs.

The rejected items reveal a pattern but not a structured order: boxes half full of sanitary napkins; reading lamps with long swinging arms in chipped enamel white, yellow, black or deep red; books of unequal sizes and thickness, mostly paperbacks whose subjects treat an unimaginably wide range—chem lab as well as sex manuals, trashy novels, astrological and self-help psychological handbooks, Somebody Hubbard's *Dianetics* which has sold untold millions of copies, cookbooks and diet guides, an authoritative account of anorexia nervosa, feminist histories, world guides to lesbian hangouts—odd pieces of the grandparents' 1950s furniture, many salvaged from basement playrooms, are "modernistic" hand-me-downs; uncomfortable overrated chic imitation Bauhaus chairs; an occasional love-seat whose arms with cigarette burns have been worn thin; small unfinished tables; Mom's bureau with rings from coffee cups, a leftover of an earlier generation from a four-year-stay in Poughkeepsie. These objects have been thrown on the pile of vanities without apparent rhyme or reason, while plastic sacks crammed with half-worn shoes and clothing were also heaped up on the dumpster not without effort. Also to be found: partially consumed foodstuffs of considerable diversity, mostly purchased from the University Market around the corner.

On the days immediately after the students' clean-up and clear-out ritual, a substantial number of whom are Americanized Asians whose parents arrive in well-groomed station wagons to transport the more precious possessions back home, a drama unfolds at the dumpster. The trash is rigorously sifted over by teams of scavengers. In a Chaplinesque footnote to the violent ravishing of the dumpster, a well-dressed, middle-aged professorial type, plainly from central Europe, may be seen lowering to his gray-haired colleague a menses-stained mattress that they sheepishly cart off to their university-owned apartment on the next block, presumably for the bed in the guest room. It is amazing what they throw out in Amerika, it will serve in good stead for the visiting artist scheduled to arrive next semester from

Poland who will read his poetry in his wife's impossible English translation.

Household items, including discarded AM-FM digital clock radios, are quickly grabbed up by what can be best defined as "independent street merchants" who occupy Casbah-like sidewalk spaces up on the broad avenue, the longest in the city, around the corner. Before long, the indiscriminately discarded objects are carefully, even lovingly, laid out on filthy blankets recovered from previous raids, priced for quick sale "as is," in an efficiently and ecologically sound, if unsuspected, underground recycling system. Any number of independent booksellers do business up there on that avenue full of bearded intellectuals with their volumes featuring more popular items like art books, do-it-yourself guides on all subjects from sexual intercourse to home plumbing repairs, together with outdated but relatively recent weekly magazines displayed with imagination and creativity. (Who buys a month-old *Newsweek* is beyond my comprehension.) The booksellers, like their counterparts on Madison Avenue, also carry a line of prints and an occasional painting, reproductions of Walt Kuhn clowns painted in the 1930s or a bridge at Arles by Vincent. Wearing apparel that was abundant in the dumpster on going-home days is now hung on colored plastic, wire or wooden hangers of incongruous sizes, all salvaged from the rubble heap or garbage from someplace nearby, at least from the neighborhood. Perhaps these merchants stand on a slightly higher rung on the social ladder than the book dealers who, along with the furniture sellers, have doggedly dusted and "restored" their minimally salable merchandise which they have sprayed with Johnson's Furniture Wax. If they fail to sell out in a day or two, their losses are trimmed by abandoning the entire stock to the Sanitation Department for the final solution, since they cannot leave their "shops" untended and a hard rain might end the affair altogether. Ironically, in an unpredictable twist, occasionally the new tenants of the dorms who arrive bright-eyed in the fall end up buying items that have been thrown out by their sisters the previous May and conceivably might actually return to the same room where they lived for as many as four years. Even an unsuspecting, unsophisticated new graduate student from Michigan who is beginning his PhD on modern Soviet History ends up with a standing lamp and a small rug from a sidewalk bodega.

Perfectly salvageable food items are found in respectable quantities in the dumpster, which had been picked over by another set of entrepreneurs. They carefully organize their finds on the flaking green edge, arranged by category; instant coffee jars appear to be the single most common item, evenly balanced between regular and caffeine-free, but small tins of lemon pepper and herbs together with dietetic produce of wide invention are all on the road to a second life. Junk foods are much less in evidence than could have been anticipated, either because they were all eaten up in one shot by the bulimic sophomore or a change seems to be taking place among young people who tend to consume healthier foods, fruit yogurt and the like. Exactly how these partial rations were disposed of remains something of a mystery; perhaps they are sold to local restaurants where the next generation of students tends to eat. More likely still, they are consumed by their finders over the next months or given out to their friends and relatives. No matter: no one can complain these items were wasted.

Bobbie's House

On the southwestern corner, hardly forty yards from the dumpster, straight up the hill from the splendid Parisian tree-lined esplanade running parallel to the river where the mattress-professor lives, stands Bobbie's house. A few steps from the entrance, there is an ex-Chock Full O' Nuts, temporarily transformed into a Korean soda fountain-cum-hamburger joint in imitation of the Peppermint Lounge of the Fifties, and finally, a discreet, cheap and enormously successful Chinese restaurant that is always jammed, and which bridges two worlds by serving "Western" breakfasts of pancakes and maple syrup along with the full Cantonese menu. The shabby forest-green wooden slats of the past were replaced by Tudor brown metal siding, except that on the south wall unpainted heavy-gauge plywood was applied, into which a makeshift front door was cut. I cannot imagine who arranged for the renovations or the motivation behind such a significant modernization. Perhaps the stand was used in the distant past as part of a program to help the handicapped or injured war veterans. It is currently occupied the now middle-aged Bobbie, a short (only four feet eleven) light skinned man who, by a quirk of contemporary usage is called "black" or "Afro-American," with dreadful eyesight, perhaps even legally blind, and who has a severe weight problem. Bobbie's stand does not have a true selection of newspapers for sale, only the *Times,* the *Daily News,* the *Post* and, out of ethnic loyalty, the *Amsterdam News,* none in excessive number nor available each day. Instead of selling out at midday, the haphazardly arranged piles of the current issues are still there throughout the afternoon, late enough so that unpunctual risers, mainly depressed college students who spend long daytime hours in the sack, can find the morning paper with the sports section intact, long after the competition has sold out. In other words, Bobbie's is hardly a thriving business, but it is home! In fact, as far as anyone knows he sleeps there with an unlikely couple as tenants who occasionally help run the business, not that space is abundant. He enjoys the comfort of electricity (is there a meter or is it siphoned off from the line for the stoplight on the corner?). He could run a small TV and a hot plate, although Bobbie himself is addicted to the take-out creamy coffee from the ex-Chock Full O' Nuts. I am constantly puzzled about toilet facilities in Bobbie's house. Have they invented a portable contraption or do they have to hold out on the long walk down to the park?

Neighborhood rumor, based largely on hearsay, has it that the rather taciturn Bobbie gathers his daily supply of newspapers in the wee hours by filching them from the stacks tossed from anxious delivery trucks near the still-closed stores, the official outlets, one might say. Another technique he is thought to employ is to "buy" for 50 cents a single issue of the *Times* from one of the vending machines at the bottom of the hill and take a handful of extras in the bargain. Both of these suggestions may be damnable lies; no one has proof of anything, although I did once see him buy the *Times* from the machine.

Bobbie's place has been spared the graffiti that typify the general area, especially on temporary storefronts and boarded up, abandoned shops, but also upon the lower reaches of the robust apartment building facades constructed in the 1910s and 1920s. The same irresistible urge to throw stones at the window panes of empty houses seems to feed the phenomenon of writing on walls, an ancient practice that has exploded into a modern plague, with a certain connivance from the art community. Ghetto youths whose canvasses are any handy surface and particularly the entire rolling stock of the mass transportation system spray their personal frustrations with more or less skill throughout the city. The resulting colored marks have been interpreted, along with crumbled automobiles and enlarged comic strip representations, as artistic contributions and have achieved official endorsement as high art. They have received the ultimate, bottom-line accolade: high prices on the auction block.

Bobbie's house is not safe, however, from the Xeroxed $8^{1}/_{2}$ x 11 inch colored sheets posted with little tear-out tabs that contain the phone numbers of persons looking for apartment shares, selling a sofa bed, announcements for self help groups, poetry readings, part-time jobs to care for an incontinent elderly handicapped man, discount computer distributors, gay/lesbian societies, language lessons by native speakers, or baby-sitters offering their services. Pasted and patched to the plywood wall of the newsstand, they evolve organically into a community bulletin board that, though not as varied as the one in the Copy Center two blocks south, may be more effective and is certainly more prestigious. As an assembly of images, they repeat themselves minimalistically, while the compositions of the individual sheets, when added together, offer an orderly display within the context of the crowded disorder of the city. Yet within their circumscribed range of possibilities in the kind, size and color of the paper used, their diversity and individuality is readily apparent. The notices are often written by hand rather than typed or set on a word processor, scrawled for clarity's sake in the labored script or even primitive block writing that recalls first grade exercises. The quality of the line or stroke, the thickness, the choice of media—fine pen, blunt pencil, or marker—emphasize ingenious diversity that is also reinforced by the technique of attaching the sheets with scotch tape, tacks, rubber cement, Elmer's Glue, or more sloppily, with that ubiquitous silver-colored duct tape.

The social function of these makeshift bulletin boards is often decisive in the lives of city dwellers. When the traditional network of relatives, friends and friends of friends is ineffectual, especially for newcomers to the city or neophytes to a particular neighborhood, unofficial, non-commercial modes of communication have a place. Most of all in the context of perception, the bulletin board has a unique visual profile, the result of a team effort, which is repeated all over the city, and is a familiar sight.

The Bus Shelter

Messages are also attached to the U-shaped bus shelter for the M104 and the M4 lines, the latter distinguished by its confusing course, which meanders downtown across 110th Street, then to Fifth Avenue, and is a prime route of passage from West to East. From time to time, usually on sweaty humid summer nights, the shelter, located a few steps from Bobbie's house, is battered to near death. The large glass partitions during these occasions are systematically flagellated, leaving intact only the cardboard inserts advertising a filtered, low tar, low nicotine cigarette. Ironically, the little metal plaque upon which is written: "Shelter No. A M-1246-14. To report damage to this shelter call (212) 669-7777. Give Shelter and ID number. Department of General Services" withstands all onslaughts except total war. Fragments of broken safety glass, cousins to those of the violated autos in the area, recall the chipped ice beneath the fresh fish and shrimps at the University Food Market. On the morning I happen upon the scene, a city employee, like a surrogate environmental artist, has wrapped the ruin in a orange-colored plastic ribbon that glows in the dark to alert passersby of the danger. Following such incidents, which may be Mafia-inspired to create plenty of business for the repair companies or merely the consequence of the utter frustration of a semi-demented citizen after a sleepless night, the cleanup occurs in a matter of days. The metal structure, with its posts and roof still functional, is eventually repaired, only to be subjected to another life and death attack, like battered wives and abused children in an incurable cycle of violence that is passed on to the generations. Out of habit people continue to stand under the wreck during the interim phase while awaiting the arrival of those noisy, smoky dragons that will carry them downtown in their bellies and spit them out like modern Jonahs at Times Square.

The College News Shop

Almost directly behind the bus stop with its mangled shelter stands the College News Shop. Cars and trucks inevitably double, sometimes triple park out front, making the morose, demoralized bus drivers' task acrobatic, besides provoking screeching bottlenecks and general distress. Tied with yellowish imitation Indian hemp, actually of plastic, the sloppy bundles of newspapers deposited helter-skelter on the left of the store's entrance, right side up, upside down or sideways lie in an interesting haphazard configuration that one might encounter on the highly polished 100–year–old wooden floors of a SoHo gallery. They more closely resemble blocks of machine-reaped hay than anything one will find before opening hours on that wide avenue. The shop does not merely stock the local dailies but the major nationals as well, including *The Washington Post* and *The Los Angeles Times*, *USA Today*, not to mention a smattering of foreign papers: *The London Times* and *The Independent*, *The Herald Tribune*, *The Frankfurter Allegemeine Zeitung*, Rome's *La Repubblica*, Paris' *Le Figaro* and a Tokyo daily—all of which can be purchased one day after issue. The availability of these newspapers in a residential neighborhood is a reminder of the international character that typifies contemporary life in New York City.

In addition to the traditional immigration patterns of the past century, a new breed has appeared notably in the past two decades. An appreciable number of Western Europeans and Japanese from international banks and corporations have come to live in America, often congregating in the metropolitan New York region. Mainly businessmen with their families, they live in unspecified overlapping colonies, often have native language schools for their children and consistently maintain connections with their countries of origin, as the English and Americans who once lived in Florence or Paris did.

At the same time this substantial and essentially well-heeled population is leaving its own mark on city life, as they, in turn, are absorbing the American experience. They participate in the cultural life of the city, tending to operate within the periphery of institutes run by the governments of their native countries; they congregate at events in some way related to them: concerts, art exhibitions, and symposia, the official visits of their intellectual and ever-present politicians.

A general stationery supplier as well as the news shop, Bobbie's nearest competitor sells computer supplies, including the somewhat outmoded type of floppy disk upon which this text is being processed. The cashier, a strikingly rude, deeply unhappy middle-aged female employee is barricaded behind rows of candy, gum, and cough drops that greet the customer purchasing his morning newspaper and, notwithstanding the guilt, a package of cigarettes. In the store's previous life, it was known as the College Smoke Shop, and the two partners who founded it and who died miserable smoking-related deaths, were themselves avid cigar smokers. They continuously played classical music on the stereo amid the fragrance of their constantly lit hand-rolled Havanas. Now the black and white daily papers, as well as the insidiously colored ones are displayed within the context of an endless array of inviting little candy packages, like the pink of Good and Plenty or five-colored Chuckles.

For many in the neighborhood, each new day is introduced by either a somewhat shy and depressed Bobbie who feels with his flabby, square hand the coins he receives in exchange for the papers that he barely sees, or by the several unpleasant words mouthed by the News Shop clerk protected by menacing candies. They exhibit myriad shapes and sizes: perfect circles, some with holes in them proportional with their outer dimensions, measured squares, golden rectangles, licorice twisted according to the Fibonacci spiral, and colors determined by marketing experts who have advanced university degrees in psychology and in color charts. They are wrapped in silver papers and golden wrappers like the objects for which an Indian chief swapped Manhattan.

The Trees

Slightly to the south and mid-block between the News Shop and the expanded University Food Market, in earlier days called the "College Take Home," a young man stands near a scruffy tree seeking handouts. Having reached his goal at the moment that I appear on the scene, some modest total for a particular need calculated to the penny, he races off past Bobbie's house on yellow and black untied, ghetto-chic Pumas, ducking into the subway entrance on the other side of the cross street to the north. I have come to realize that when people ask for money on the street claiming to be hungry, they very well may be hungry, although for most of us on the other side of the socio-economic divide such a condition would constitute a novel experience excepting, of course, for pathological anorexics. Some of the beggars only pretend to be hungry to get the needed cash for a pint of sweet wine or a fix. Yet the generalization holds, supported by the length of the lines where food is provided free, especially at the Methodist Church's soup kitchen a couple of blocks to the south; the clients often congregate hours ahead of time to be sure to be served as soon as possible, and probably because they haven't anything else to do anyway. Besides, who would eat garbage, a common occurrence in the city, if they were not hungry? Fade out such an awful thought. In times past the poor privately ate canned dog food as regular fare and the practice may still hold. And if that awful statement is really true, the proliferation of tastes and flavors in which they come would be explained.

The trinity of trees planted three years previously at the edge of the sidewalk may belong to the beech family; about eleven feet tall, the skinny but hardy bastards still wear their original nursery-applied burlap coats which from sheer neglect were never removed, even during the heat wave last August, when the temperature broke 96° six days in a row. Supported by two unequal sticks forced into the nearly impervious ground and tied with rusting wire, two of them are shielded from urinating dogs whose irritating acid would do any tree in after a while. And, after all, a law requiring that owners pick up their pets' liquid wastes would be mind-boggling to enforce. The low black fences are composed of two rows of continuous intersecting arches, one about six inches higher than the other, embedded into a frame of flat metal raised slightly above the level of the sidewalk. The third tree, as if to avoid monotony or because an anonymous civil servant in a remote office in Brooklyn forgot to process the purchase order, was entirely unguarded; nonetheless it seems to thrive like the others on the combination of soot, truck and bus fumes and morbid irrigation consisting of filthy rains and pockmarked slushy ice. Garbage bags surround the trees, even the fenced in ones, functioning like lumpy but massively out of proportion black or brown articulated bases for the skinny, gloomy columns.

Down the cross street toward the river nearly in front of the women's college residence hall, similar trees are bedded in a little private plot, each with plantings of carefully disposed, flowering annuals, flourish until the beginning of November some years. Thanks to the greenhouse effect, they may soon bloom till Christmas, an indication of the essential fertility of New York's native soil that is further evidenced by the lush but disorderly growth in the miles-long narrow park beside the river. Obviously, the trees up on that broad way suffer from the same malaise as do the human inhabitants, from greater abuse, more rumpus and noise than their companions, who grow faster and are noticeably less abused and are surely less neurotic in their idyllic setting along the river bank.

The Trash Cans

By established tradition, fixed at the northwestern corner of the block and, in fact, on every corner on that north-south passageway, hardly a couple of yards in real distance from the delicacies of the delicatessen counter inside the University Food Market, is the ubiquitous wicker-like, silvery trash container, one among tens of thousands, maybe even a million of this intrinsically faulty model on duty throughout the city. Once a style or pattern is set, as with these ugly inefficient receptacles, even a world war is insufficient impetus to change. Although reasonably new, the one by the market is already tortured by ill-treatment, no longer possessing its aboriginal cylindrical form. An attached text warns of a $100 fine for putting regular (i.e., "live") garbage there, a meaningless but well-intentioned admonition to apartment house residents whose own receptacles are full and who have no place for their refuse. Although only half-full on the particular morning that I choose to take notice, an oddity since the contents usually overflow the rim, the entire immediate surroundings are incorporated with it and form a still-life construction, rich in private and public iconographies.

Obviously scavengers had sifted through the contents during the night, although in this category of street operation no fixed schedule is ever strictly maintained, with the proviso that some of the collectors are slightly embarrassed for themselves and, possibly, for the conscience of the entire community, and thus work unobserved at night. Scattered like confetti, broken orange skins with their artificially acrylic-bright patination applied on an assumption reached decades ago and never again questioned that an orange had to be orange and not green in order to market the product. A crumbled transparent sheet of what once was called wax paper that accompanies pizza slices sold down the block to the south had traces of tomato sauce, a flick or two of hot pepper seeds, and a trace of powdered garlic. Often the trash cans yield perfectly "good" half-eaten segments of the Italian flat pies tossed out by customers who couldn't eat what they were momentarily induced to purchase, or guilt-ridden dieters with second thoughts. These morsels were grabbed up in the second round by hungry street people along with other half-eaten items.

All the returnable cans and bottles had been cherry-picked, as happens to nearly all the exposed city garbage, including containers located on the campus of the great university on the other side of the avenue from Bobbie's house. Since the deposit is so slight, most people calculate it in the cost and chuck away the container without a second thought. But the down and outers can make an almost-decent wage and an honest piece of change with the empties, provided they are not overcome by the smells they need to endure, as required by the nature of their hunt. Furthermore, they must tolerate hostile storekeepers who are reluctant to accept the empty cans and bottles. Here is another of the mysterious cycles of distribution of goods and services operating in the city which planners never foresaw.

The unpredicted process has the unsavory side effect of spilling garbage out into the public paths. Happily, the mess is faded out pretty fast from consciousness but remains buried somewhere in a backup file under the heading of urban experience. Since the five-cent cans are buried in black plastic shrouds, the scavengers inevitably must break them open in order to extract their modest aluminum treasures; in the process they cause havoc and untold extra work for the porters of the apartment buildings as well as the store owners. With the sacks slit open, when the garbage is finally collected, every sort of unappetizing and often quite private refuse flops onto the sidewalks and has to be swept away in still another bout in the apparently unending disposal process, so that instead of relief when the smelly messes are lifted away to the noisy scows, there is a fairly demoralizing aftermath. Those in the deposit business are essentially specialists, tending to leave for another wave of practitioner possibly desirable items, which means that the garbage is picked over again, with more spillage, and increased discomfort. Why the social forces haven't devised a better solution than these disruptive attacks upon the city's garbage baffles me. I don't understand why building supers continue to put out the waste in the evenings so that the scavengers have a solid twelve hours to do their work, as well as the procedure whereby deposit bottles and cans are supposed to be left in a separate place.

Unlike the black disposal sacks belched up from the basements and laid out beside the service entrances of the apartment buildings, the wire trash cans readily reveal their basic holdings. One early morning a perfectly decent looking pair of Nikes had been picked out, the worst of the refuse cleaned off and neatly placed together on the filthy surface at an oblique angle near the edge of the curb, a found object displayed for public viewing. The original finder of the sneakers must have taken their measure, found that the size was not right and invitingly left them for someone else in an act of uncalculated generosity.

On blowy mornings, the scene is truly hellish, especially after a rain which one might hope would produce a cleansing effect: instead it manages to move the filth around some. Slowly as the sun rises, the walks are swept, a certain effort is made to tidy up, but the smells and the memories of the filth, which are never entirely eliminated, become a mounting reality in the course of the subsequent hours. Indeed, along with urban sounds, these odors constitute still another contextual element in the city. Different grease smells well up from restaurants: beef grease from hamburger joints (Happy Burger is a well chosen name); peanut oil grease from Chinese ones; special odors from the Middle East specialists, and so on, and all are funneled onto the sidewalk through noisy air conditioning ducts into the eyes and noses of the pedestrians. Combined with the rather invisible automobile fumes and the waves of all-too-visible diesel fumes from trucks and buses, a noxious mixture, mighty tough to switch off, ensues.

The trash container's loyal companion is the usually red, white and blue mail box, although it is sometimes all green. The form has remained pretty much the same for half a century, but it too is now subjected to graffiti and more especially to the application of small posters and other signifiers, much like the bulletin board at Bobbie's. It has suffered various indignities along with the bus stop shelter, but has been repeatedly reconditioned, repainted and put back into service; the mail box has a gigantic paunch and a wide, voracious mouth that is usually clogged up to the gullet so that down its throat one force feeds the telephone and Con Ed bills.

Chapter III.
Food and Contemporary Society

Food and the immense infrastructure of affiliated activities occupy a substantial portion in any given day in any given week for most members of a modern society, for city dwellers, suburbanites and country folk alike. An intricate industry in which not only the actual production, preparation, packaging and selling are part of the system but the advertising and promotion as well. In addition, the entire world of activities connected with the effects of eating too little, too much, and/or the wrong things, plus the myriad illnesses that result from consumption, their prevention and cure are all necessary ingredients of the whole collage. Within the anatomy of its widest definition, food represents an indicative conglomerate of factors related to modern life. Considered through the lens of its applicable spin-offs, food offers crucial and otherwise unobtainable insights into organized society's very core and, consequently, into all its activities, including a highly representative area: art. In early times and still today in less developed cultures and as a survival in more developed ones, open markets flourished, where what was sold was chiefly what was grown or processed nearby, without many intervening stages. On that basic level, stacked in appetizing and aesthetically rewarding mounds and in cool bins either in produce stores or in appropriate sections of supermarkets, fresh vegetables and fruits are still offered nostalgically, for sale in more or less the old way, although Saranwrapped plastic trays are common, too. These items now come usually from far away places: California or Florida, Chile and Mexico, Israel, Holland and Spain. Grown in vast mechanized factory-farms and never harvested by the owner of the land, they have been treated as products— refrigerated, coated with preservatives, waxed, perhaps gassed, and certainly, sprayed with pesticides and irradiated. The odyssey from grower to consumers for such products can be juxtaposed with traditional modes that continue to be reflected in farm stands in rural areas and even in the city at so-called farmer's markets that are set up on fall weekends in shabby empty lots, spruced up for the occasion.

One of the changes in eating habits that has occurred in modern society that vastly differs from past practice is the complete loss of a sense of the seasons, recaptured only occasionally by jaunts to the countryside where one can buy and even pick apples in September and October, corn in July and August, depending upon the local climate conditions. Lost is the expectation of each harvest with its pleasure and excitement: the earliest tender lettuce and the first crop of white-tipped French radishes that heralded the spring; then came the fruit, sweet cherries and peaches, the different varieties of apples as they ripened, usually beginning with the uninspiring Macs; later came the Concord grapes and pears. The reaping of the vegetables finally ended with cauliflower and the hearty gigantic red cabbages. There was a time for walnuts and another for chestnuts. Olives can be harvested as late of December and even January in Monte Rinaldo if there has not been a deep freeze.

All in its season is a rule of life that has virtually disappeared. One finds almost everything at every time of the year and not merely in super-refined specialty shops. The joy of even recalling the habits of home preserving when quart jars of delicious apricots in a natural liquid were brought out on birthdays and the like as homage to the previous season's generosity is all but a lost delight. No doubt people continue freezing and canning, but not the city folks, who eat spiritless cherries from Chile all winter and dreadful plastic hothouse tomatoes from Holland (of all places!) twelve months a tasteless year.

The conditions surrounding the selling of foodstuffs vary substantially from item to item, stage to stage and from place to place. The industries occupied with the processing of food, dried, frozen, precooked, cured, canned, bottled, baked, boxed are merely the most visible aspects of a vast enterprise. The costly and usually effective marketing of food products plays a major part in the entire operation as does packaging, a relatively new activity (who would want to call it an "art"?). Design, illustration, graphics, color separations, lettering, rendering and photography go into packaging, which is regarded as vital for the selection of products at the point of sale.

The various hookups for distribution, with armies of salespeople from every level, computer connections, contests, inventory, products, consumers, color, and taste control. Public relations staffs and advertising agencies that propagandize the products constitute another facet of the food business, one in which the product sold has virtually no rapport with its presentation or with claims broadcast on its behalf. The advertising of food products is crucial to the success or failure of daily newspapers, and even weekly and monthly magazines around the

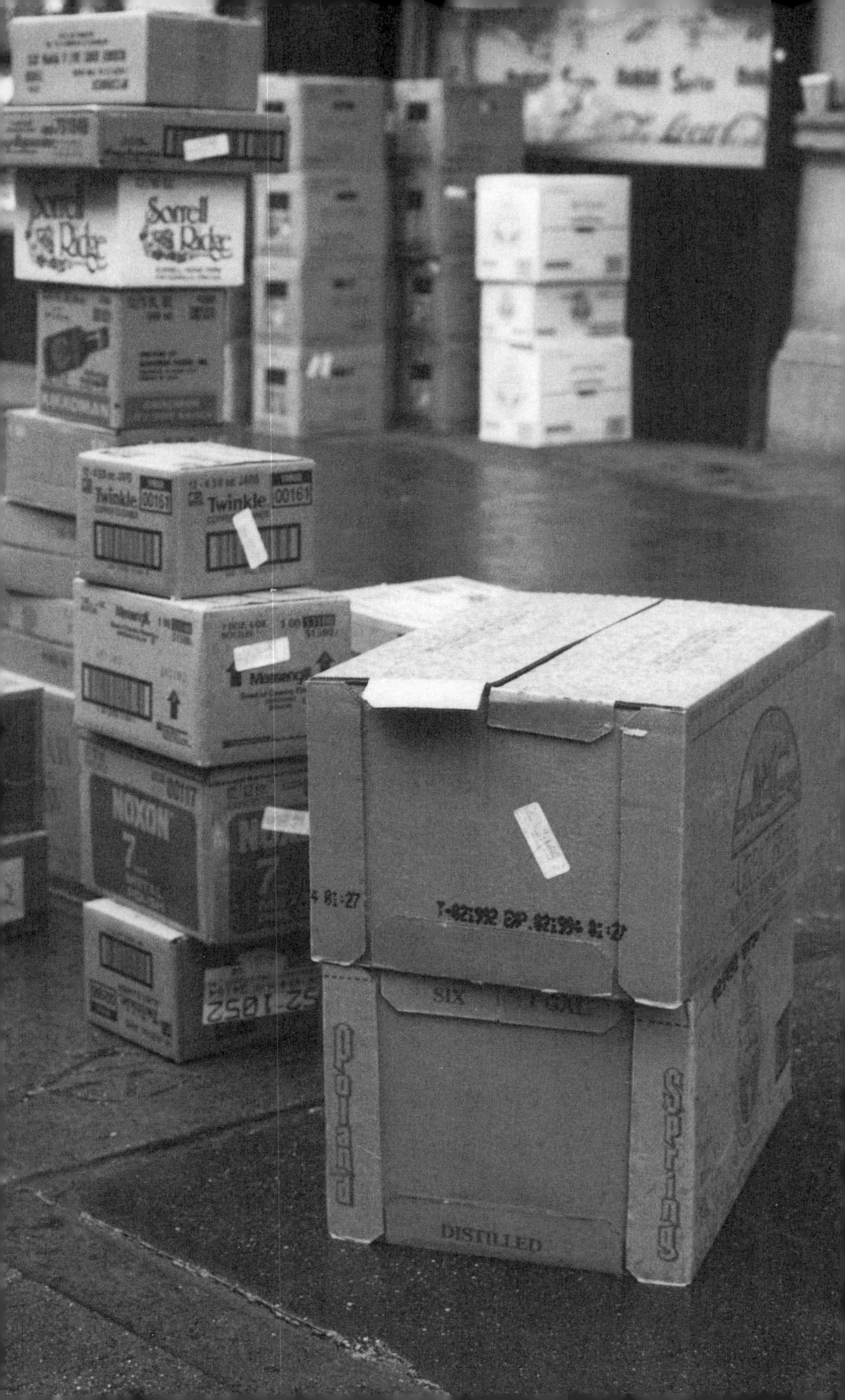

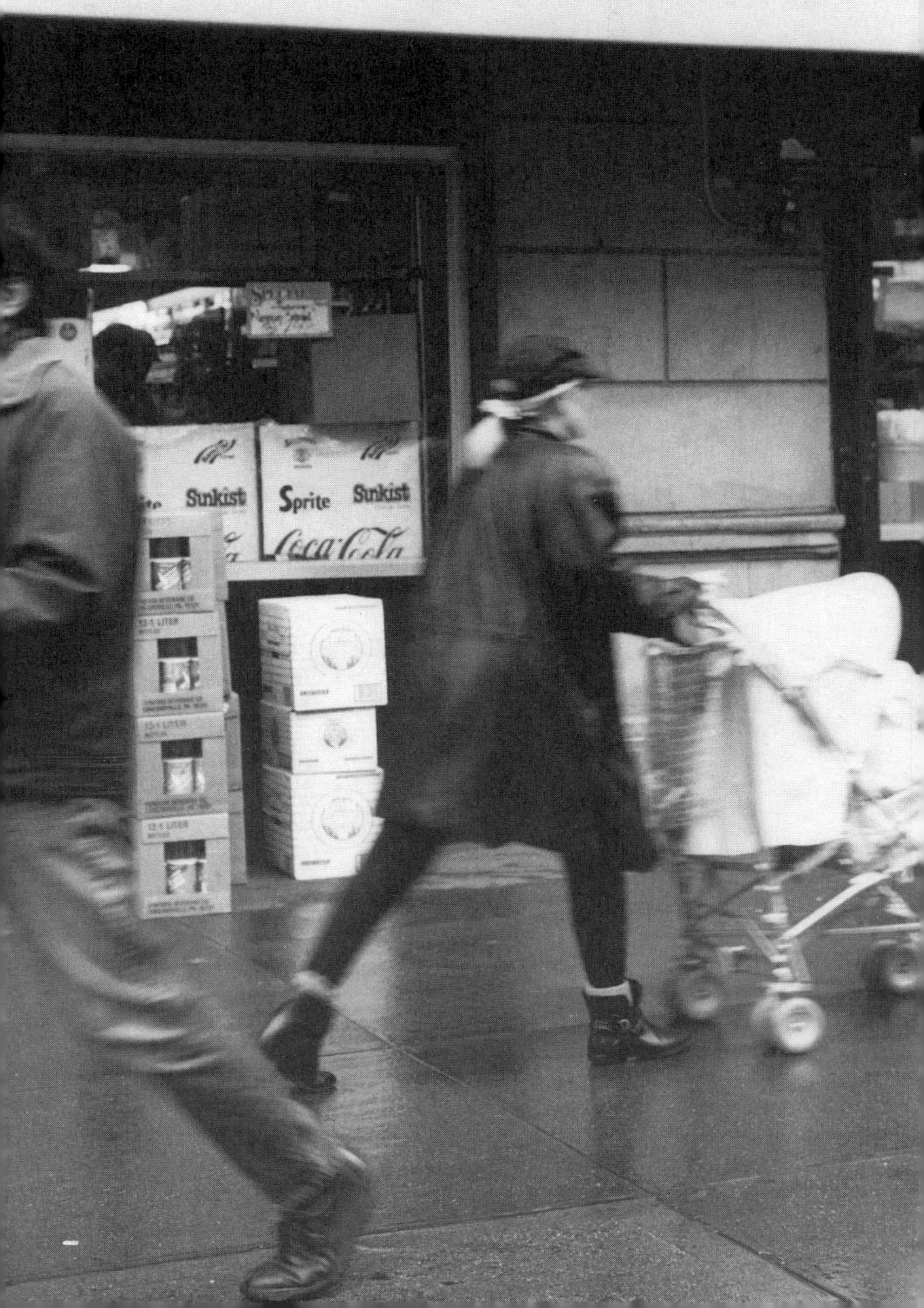

UNIVERSITY F
Sunkist
Sprite
Sunkist
Coca-Cola

country depend heavily on revenue from such promotions. Popular magazines reveal the extent to which direct food advertising profiles such publications—page after page of enticing displays, either in color or black and white—especially when we consider that beverages must be included as a part of the food equation. But in the reading matter too, with diets and recipes forming regular features, food stands along with sex, explicitly and implicitly, as a cornerstone theme.

The wide use of coupons in America, a plague which has spread to the rest of the Western world, deserves special mention not merely because of its time-consuming dimension but because of the complexity it adds to the act of shopping. Several categories of the Monopoly game gone balmy may be distinguished, including those coupons which are valid only in a given store or those given chain of stores and whose redemption is limited to a single day or a single week. They may offer a dollar off on an item, on the total amount of money spent, or perhaps a free can, of what else?, tomato soup, all limited to a fixed amount per household, although husbands and wives are easily spotted divvying up the groceries to achieve the needed amount twice.

Intelligent shoppers are required to think through the varying, sometimes conflicting conditions of the store coupon which are then either cut out with scissors or, by the more impulsive, torn along the dotted lines as best one can. Another category includes a raft of radiantly colored manufacturers' coupons, whose endless qualifications and "whereas-es" in fine print is as confusing as one's Federal Income Tax or home owners insurance policy. They may come in the mail in miscellaneous packets or found in magazines and newspapers organized by direct-mail advertising specialists; alternately, coupons are buried right there in the box of Kellogg's Corn Flakes and dry cat food. If collected with care, as millions of economy-minded homemakers do, the actual monetary savings can be significant. Imitation leather wallets and separators have been designed specially as holders for the purpose of organizing the coupons into categories with attention to the dates of expiration, segregating also those that have to be sent directly to the manufacturer from those that are to be turned in at the store, all of which requires the skill of a trained museum curator. Since the popularization of these scraps, "clipping coupons" has taken on a new and more egalitarian meaning; it is mini-industry in itself but also a ridiculous and oppressively time-consuming activity, one in which the poor, who are often unable to follow all of the intricacies, are penalized. Nor should one lose sight of the fact that coupons are another of those widely disseminated, colorful printed objects, like money, offering two-dimensional experiences that have a unique iconography combining a word text and imagery and yet retaining a calculable monetary value.

Popular, mass-oriented publications are filled with articles on restaurants, what and where to eat in exotic lands, on fitness, and endless weight-loss plans and diet suggestions, as well as advertisements of products directed to fulfill the dietary programs. In book publishing, too, we find issues surrounding food, weight loss, weight gain, diseases related to food consumption, proper eating habits and improper ones, the parameters of which appear to shift every few years, medical books that emphasize food and health, Polish-

Jewish cookbooks or those advocating macrobiotic meals based upon seaweed and brown rice. If we then momentarily turn to the most encompassing medium for entertainment and information gathering on the part of the larger public, television, the extent to which food and food-related questions occupy the screens of America proves to be overwhelming.

Undeniably, then, aspects of food have a commanding position within the modern social picture and provide one of the best places to observe patterns that, in turn, can illuminate basic cultural choices. The most convenient place to obtain a handle on these patterns is the retail outlet, where most of the purchasing occurs. The one nearest my home is called the University Food Market. Stylistically unique features above and beyond the individual personality of the store (every one has a "style" of its own, reflecting a combination of the demands of the clientele and the outlook of the manager, somewhat like an art gallery) can serve as a link to wider conclusions.

The University Food Market

The owners of the University Food Market, a mecca for both the affluent and the poor residents in the neighborhood, have private gold mine. They are keenly, even brilliantly, aware of the desires of their patrons, composed of an odd concoction of university instructors, staff, and students who come from all over the country and the world, and the normal West Side resident unaffiliated with the university. District storekeepers have jealously calculated that the amount of business per square foot rivals that of Bloomingdale's, which was the apex in the generation of the 1960s-1980s span.

Historically, the store, which previous to an expansion and renovation a few years back, was a nondescript student-oriented take-out deli that could be found in a hundred other college areas, now occupies about forty percent of the block's frontage, though in depth it is rather shallow. Always busy and frequently jammed to capacity, the store opens rather late as these things go, at 8 AM. By then, customers, mainly uniformed—campus guards, maintenance workers, city policeman and sanitation workers—are lined up for their coffee and sweet rolls "to go" Trucks have been standing out front, motors on to keep warm in winter and to generate the refrigerators in summer, and thus fouling the communal lungs in all seasons as they aliment the neighborhood's bellies. In every imaginable shape, in diverse hues and with special lettering and decorations on their sides, they are double-parked to leave the lane nearest the curb free for the mechanized sweeper whose major task seems to be to relocate dampened dirt from the curb towards the central stage of the street, between the hours 8 and 9 each weekday morning.

Now a desperate scene of shifting cars unfolds because tickets are given with relish to those offenders who are caught blocking the path of the sweeper. Store keepers run in and out, and all of them have home-made signs on the dashboard indicating their identities; then for the remainder of the day they are safe, making ready for the dreary trip back to Bergen Country, after feeding quarters to the greedy meters throughout the day.

Each weekday morning foodstuffs in stacks of as many as six cartons high, including the ubiquitous Campbell's Tomato Soup and towers of

Tropicana Orange Juice, Ballantine's Ale, Kellogg's Corn Flakes and hillocks of others, including household products like Brillo, grace the spacious sidewalk of that broad avenue near a great but declining university, arranged in a tortuous maze of mini-turrets, as they might be on the ground floor of the Guggenheim Museum. The pedestrians trying to move either north or south must negotiate the labyrinthine walls of cartons, temporarily resting there on their way to the market's dingy, roach-ridden basement. The boxes are eventually tossed via a metal slide with slick shiny wheels that have been polished from constant use into the mouth of a yawning, iron-enframed opening in the sidewalk, part of the circuitous route toward consumption. Inside the store, they will be belched up in an awkward lift, when, by two-way radio clicking on and off, the vaguely ambivalent manager, a pretentious but efficient sergeant with a thousand keys on a stout ring tucked beneath his stout paunch who shouts his needs at the good-looking Puerto Rican boys, not without affection: "Vita Herring in sour cream, 4 oz. Lets move."

One enters the University Market through an unpretentiously narrow gate with an automatic sliding door that clicks open and then closed as one leaves, activated by an electric eye. Inside, where closed circuit TV keeps a constant Big Brother eye out for shoplifters, an entire world of potentialities for no-nonsense eating unfolds, at variance with conventional supermarkets not merely in terms of its reduced size but in orientation, or if you wish, "style." While the megastores cater to the family-centered customer, younger married people with two kids and where shopping has a fair-like quality, the market near the great international university appeals to the no nonsense childless married or unmarried couples and singles, although a reduced selection of baby foods is directed at the handful of neighborhood infants as well as the occasional depressed, incontinent geriatric customer. In the same category are oppressive Pampers, presumably an amalgam of paper and plastic that has thoroughly replaced those cloth ones distributed by the "Diaper Service," which twice a week brought a soft pile folded into squares and wrapped in brown paper, removing the smelly but somehow wholesome collection from the previous delivery. Now, all the baby doo-doo and urine mixed with Johnson's Baby Oil and sticky talc is fed into the vast disposal operation to stifle the world, insidiously compacted and packaged, collected, trucked, barged out of sight, conveniently switched off. Pampers may not be any more ecologically harmful than a good many other items offered at the market, but they are symbolic, perpetually reminding us from birth that we are literally choking ourselves in our own refuse.

Pet foods also have a prominent presence in the market: city inhabitants are animal lovers, almost by definition. An isolated, lonely, impersonal life can be mitigated by the loyal pampered pet who, sometimes for a decade or more, is a widow's only companion. One such woman in the neighborhood, bent over by 90 degrees which happens to corresponds to the number of years she has spent on this earth, has an ancient frail little nondescript yellowish dog whose name "College Boy" she calls out while on their arthritic constitutional through the campus each morning.

Household or drugstore items as such occupy a mere half length of aisle, in contrast to the endless corridors in their counterparts in suburban New Jersey, where even clothing, auto supplies, Water Picks, Taiwanese sneakers together with hardware, nasty packaged cast iron hammers and pliers also produced in the Orient are featured. Essentially what confronts the customer is an expanded self-service delicatessen, a modified Zabar's, Balducci's, or Grace's, where the offerings, even the pure staples like sugar and salt, are genetically gene-spliced breeds or at least treated as if they were exclusive. One can purchase sea salt rather than the common iodized table variety. There is not only an ample exhibit of liter-size imported extra virgin olive oils for the Mediterranean diet from Lamporecchio, a nondescript Tuscan town at the foot of Monte Albano a few miles from Leonardo's birthplace, but also those from Spain, California and vials for the truly discriminating cooks from the minuscule French production. Vinegars derived from Champagne and raspberry wine (to cook red radishes in) or the nearly tar-colored balsamic variation from Modena are available with a choice of brands. The point is that virtually every recognized specialty from the four corners of the earth are on the shelves in an ingeniously cabalistic configuration of mouthwatering temptations: palmettos and other hearts, like those bite size artichokes in a thick yellow/green oil.

A salad bar has been provided, allocating full recognition of contemporary preferences but not the usual one found at fast-food outlets; choices are consistent with the specialistic tone of the rest of the store, like the fresh vegetable section. Here, selected produce, carrots with the stalks still attached, Brussels sprouts in little round waxed paper baskets, long, threatening, stark white (on the inside) Chinese radishes with straggly beard-like roots, and true rarities, out-of-season cherries from Chile, imported *porcini* mushrooms from Yugoslavia, and frightfully expensive fresh figs (from where?).

Nobler still is the fresh fish counter: live lobsters crawling lazily at the bottom of their glass pre-extermination chambers, costly flounder filets and salmon slices resting proudly on finely crushed ice beds, cleaned shrimp ranging in size and price from jumbos to precooked smaller ones and sad-eyed lake trout. An active meat and poultry counter provides tailored cuts prepared-to-order merely for the asking, at no extra charge, there being plenty of charge already. A customer has ample opportunity for personalized service, although a indigenous incivility if not outright defensive rudeness is endemic to all the services supplied by the market (and the other shops in the neighborhood for that matter, except Mike whose real name is Danny, the dry cleaner). A similar condition is decidedly common in the entire city, presumably the result of the sheer quantity of customers as well as the stressful working conditions; Korean greengrocers have been quick to catch on and often outdo their native counterparts in rudeness.

The candy department, proportionally expanded in terms of the total space available, is skillfully situated close to the checkout area. A selection of Swiss chocolate bars that can hardly be rivaled at the *Migros* out on the autoroute near Lausanne with every flavor of Lindt, Callier and Tobler, plus Belgian, British and Italian boxed entries. Sweet teeth notwithstanding, the throbbing heart of the market, its *raison d'être* and its historic origins, is a long, high glass counter facing an consistent bread display where, incidentally, you cannot find a single loaf of vitamin-enriched Wonder Bread. Burlap sacks of coffee beans with black-stenciled printing that function as an engaging display are casually stacked at the end that squares off with the storefront composed of undecorated plate glass windows. Exotic blends are ground on request, providing a agreeable aroma in that corner of the store. On the fabulous cheese table laid out in front of the counter rests not a single slab of pale-orange Kraft's fabled American cheese, the nation's eponymous favorite, can be found. It has been supplanted by New York State and Vermont cheddars as well a boundless array of imports whose tonalities encompass a range of off-whites, whites on whites with the crumbly crusts contrasted with pale inner chambers, all encapsulated with glimmering transparent plastic sheets. The dried and smoked fish section is especially favored with the infinitesimally thinly sliced rarities treated with compassionate respect.

None of the items at the Deli counter, including the fish, are ever priced in the pound rations but by the "quarter," which coincides roughly with the 100 gram unit common in Europe. Westphalian ham appears less outrageously expensive as $4.99 a quarter as it would at $20.00 the [*sic*] pound. This system of pricing has become common throughout the city and in many localities of the country as well. Part of the explanation lies in the fact that the smaller unit gives the false notion that the item costs less than it really does and is therefore less immoral. Furthermore, with a large singles population the "normal" unit of purchase may well be a quarter pound anyway; in the usual course of events the single person would never buy a pound of anything, ever. Anyway, most customers of the University Market seek variety even in a single meal so they tend to buy diverse foods in small quantities as little as eighths of a pound shares. The prices in the market are generally steep, perhaps 30 percent more than the chain supermarkets located six blocks to the south (though not consistently on everything), a fact that does not appear to affect business.

Also reflective of the eating habits of the neighborhood is the extensive choice of prepared, piping-hot dishes that one can take home and eat at once: ravioli swimming in deep vermilion surroundings punctuated by globules of golden oil, noodles stained with greenish pesto, paler Scandinavian meat balls, veal stew, roast chicken. Few items at the Deli counter can be considered as strictly American. Instead, a bastardized international concoction is offered, although most recipes have been modified in their transatlantic voyage to suit local taste. At the same time combinations and mixing, intolerable in the countries or regions where the particular food originated, are unexceptional manifestations in their new circumstances. For instance, an undergraduate selects his hero sandwich on Italian bread with Italian sweet sausage in a Ragu sauce accompanied by a bag of Wise onion-flavored potato chips and a small bottle of mountain pure unfizzy Evian water from the French Alps, as a health precaution, I suppose.

Panhandlers with their crumpled paper cups who work their territory in front of and in the vicinity of the University Market are numerous all the time, six or eight regulars man their stations until the bewitching hour when action ends for the night. Nonetheless, they fare reasonably well.

Neighborhood gossip claims that they take in as much as 30 dollars a day. The singular, rather stylish and inevitably polite middle-aged black woman who sits on a stone slab that juts out from the building and is regularly on display by the store's main and only entrance, is far and away the most successful, a beneficiary of her pleasant demeanor and, besides, a generally approved embodiment of feminist sentiment in the neighborhood. She is a regular, even after having been beaten up, but with swollen face she still manages to offer everyone a wide, toothy smile. After purchasing a few slices of Norwegian lox at a hefty price and a Toblerone stick of chocolate composed of crushed nuts and honey, few clients possess the moral strength to hide an already conditioned guilt to the extent of refusing to tend a halfway decent tribute. Outright refusal seems out of the question under the circumstances, especially in the rush to get home to gobble up the goodies in sinful privacy.

A majestic man who is, as far as I know, above asking for handouts, cleans the sidewalk for the management of the market each morning. He arrives at about 8:30 with four tightly stuffed plastic jumbo shopping bags bearing the market's logo and containing his earthly belongings. His home is one of the narrow, shallow portals on the façade of the Methodist church on the next block that serve as three primary residences by night, both summer and winter. Their inhabitants lay down a double layer of cardboard to function as insulation against the dampness of the ground as well as offering a slightly resilient surface upon which to rest their bones. The human-size spaces are leftovers from the Middle Ages that have accrued a vital contemporary meaning. The man in question could easily have been a Nigerian tribal chief or shaman, who dresses with nobility, conscious of the magic of color and costume. He wears a turbaned head gear of his own invention as well as two jackets, one over the other, and a heavy sweater all buried beneath a torn, ragged cloak of many colors and of all seasons—his royal cape.

In exchange for the work performed with intense efficiency, he receives a double container of coffee, one third of which is half-and-half (a reasonably nourishing drink when four heaping spoonfuls of sugar are added), plus several "buttered," seeded rolls, which are not really buttered but coated in thick palette-knifed applications of corn oil margarine. Following his ritualistic activity and meal, the African disappears from the neighborhood; where is anybody's guess, although I think I spotted him asleep in the jungle at the edge of the sacred wide river along Riverside's steep slope.

At the six checkout counters that to the unknowing seem excessive in a place as small as the market, the customer is greeted by Hispanic women who handle transaction with noteworthy flair. There is usually a lad operating at least one of the National Cash Registers, but his line should be avoided at all costs; he can hardly compete with the women in either speed or efficiency, since he regularly has to stop and ask for prices. The "girls" are carefully made-up, clothed with self-aware elegance primed by stylish heavy gold jewelry. Though not outright unpleasant, these cashiers demonstrate little cordiality, failing even to exchange those few glad words, like the empty, oppressive "have a good day." This may actually be a blessing. Yet, one inevitably leaves the store with a faint ill feeling, exacerbated by the knowledge that panhandlers are lying in wait directly beyond the automatic sliding door.

The complexity, refinement, variety and sophistication as exemplified by the offerings at a New York City neighborhood superette, like University Food Market, represents an unparalleled modern condition. When kings and princes of times gone by sought exotic foods from distant lands, their selections were surely modest by comparison.

Today, rich and poor alike are unwilling to forgo Swiss chocolate or their Johnny Walker Black and Perrier unless a scandal over possible impurities breaks in the media. Recognizing the hold food consumption systems have over aspects of a modern society, we are encouraged to determine the impact on the population generally.This may offer, by direct application and by analogy, insights into the functioning of artistic events, and more specifically still, illuminate the implicit effect this conceivably exercises on the very foundations of modern reception and modern perception. The anarchic diversity which has been observed, coupled with an inherent incongruity between various items, participates in a central ritual of contemporary life in the United States, Canada, Western Europe and isolated pockets of the world community, that is, in areas where International Art has taken root. The point is verified by the recognition that the reverse appears to be the case in most of Eastern Europe, notwithstanding the total breakdown in Soviet hegemony and the demise of authoritarian Communist regimes. Much the same is true for the so-called Third World, as well as in the ghettoes and in specific pockets like the hills of West Virginia, where prosperity has forgotten to stop by.

In all these places, virtually no variety or choice of food is even remotely possible. Indeed, instead of sophisticated offerings of delicate appetizers, followed by an elaborate framework of courses, severe shortages of even the most monotonous foodstuffs are common. Oversize canvases constructed of a solitary field of a faintly modulated tonality, sometimes interrupted by a thin strip of another color, can hardly be expected to have a cordial reception there, unless they possess as yet undiscovered magical powers to bring manna, rain or offer desirable shade.

Fooding

In the Western countries and particularly in the United States, a substantial portion of waking hours are dedicated to food related activities, an assertion that might come as something of a surprise. Among the most obvious areas is that of actually purchasing the food to be consumed. Oddly enough, and contrary to what might be commonly thought, the act of marketing is relatively easier in the inner city than in the suburbs or in the country. Urban shops are invariably within walking distances from home, wherever that happens to be, because of the organic fashion in which neighborhoods have evolved where all basic outlets are clustered together. A pharmacy, a dry cleaner and tailor, shoemaker, a barber shop and a beauty salon, green grocers and meat markets, a bakery, general foods stores as well as a health food outlet, a florist, and a stationer with indispensable computer supplies, a hardware store, a bank branch or two, and so on, are all musts. In the city, people tend to shop more frequently, which can be regarded as a social event, but buy less on each outing.

In contrast, in ex-urban shopping centers even the supermarket fails to satisfy the total needs. In imitation of city practice, smaller specialty stores are common satellites, but since their evolution has been more artificial, the deficiencies are unmistakable. Thus, despite the comfort of the giants, you need to pay demanding visits to other malls, perhaps ten or fifteen miles away, at least if you want fresh rabbit. Besides, beyond the city limits, the automobile is a *sine qua non* which, in turn, requires an elaborate, time-wasting and expensive series of enterprises. The family car must be kept in operation not only to carry Mom to the shopping center and from one to another but to keep the entire family functioning. Wherever the shopping takes place, the actual process as well as the travel by mechanized transportation entails hours, when considering activities like check cashing and getting those cursed coupons ready for use. Besides, the more developed the level of taste, the more complicated the process of shopping seems to become.

A sensible portion of food activity, or "fooding," is devoted to preparation, which signifies merely opening a can or two and stirring the contents, or defrosting and heating same in a microwave or possibly it involves a minimal amount of real "cooking" as limited as turning out a platter of bacon and eggs. All of this requires sanctified time. When it comes to the passionate gourmet cook, or the painstaking and duty-bound mother-cook, wife-cook, husband-cook, or the husband-and-wife-cook who spend hours preparing a repast that promises to please a loved one, themselves, or guests, the amount of time expended knows no limits—plus the clean-up that is the shaggy coda to the purchase and preparation of food. Even when the chef has heavily relied upon disposable paperware and Teflon pots and pans (never as easy to clean as they are made out to be), someone must stack the dishwasher and put in the soap, unload it after the cycles have clicked off, and put away the dishes once sparkling, and finally tidy and sweep up the kitchen and take out the garbage. Naturally, in cases where a good deal of domestic help is available, presumably in the households of art dealers and their treasured collectors/patrons, for example, and less frequently in the homes of those who make art, time expended operates somewhat differently but, I suggest, preoccupation with the food operations reigns across the board.

Aside from food preparation itself, actual consumption, climax of the dinner party, occupies a substantial proportion of the waking day, whether this unfolds at home, at friends, in public restaurants and private clubs, in luncheonettes and fast food outlets, standing alongside wagons, push carts and stands on the city streets, or—an experience of increasing popularity—on foot beside a vending machine in dismal, ill-lighted corridors or refreshment areas of an office building, or at an Exxon née Esso station where you can eat on the way in or out of the rest room, without even the privilege of being insulted. On the opposite side of the fooding spectrum are those occasions when one goes to a restaurant or to friends' homes, highly gregarious events, prefaced by cocktails and large talk concluding with espresso and brandy. Here time is strung out: they say you never age while at table, but chunks of the day can be consumed along with calories and cholesterol added to the veins, not to mention those intervals wasted traveling to and from the place of eating, a sum that could mount up considerably, since people are quite disposed to

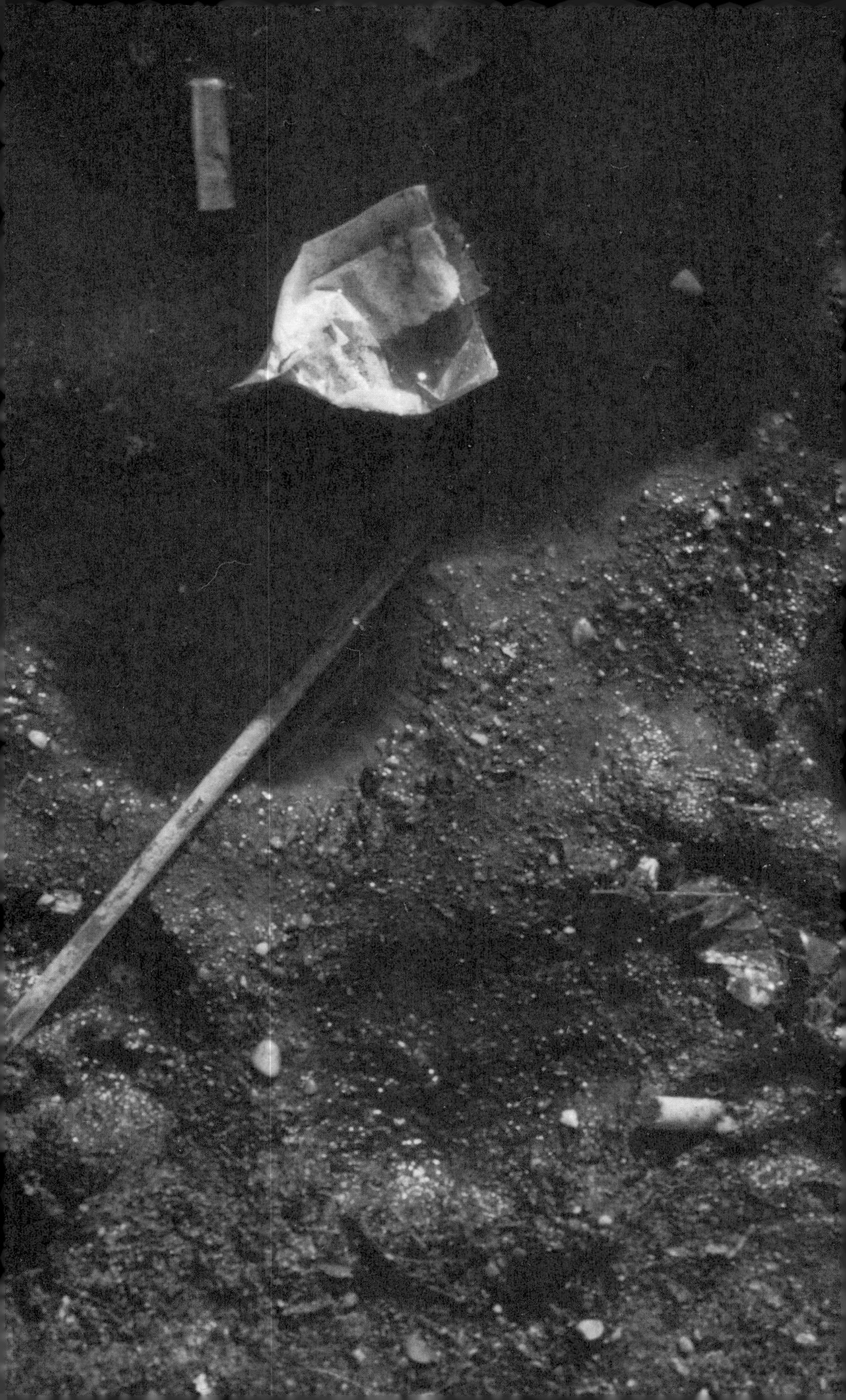

journey an hour or more for a good feed. The totals become astonishing.

For decades the vogue was to eat at drive-ins seated in the Chevy, one of the few truly sacred spots in American society, but the appeal of that, too, has faded. Drive-ins have lost much of their popularity, although without question snacking and munching continues to take place in the typical family's typical Toyota, whether it is parked or roving on the highway. More characteristic, though hardly new, are the roadside stops on thruways, autoroutes, autobahns and autostradas. The feeling in such locales is unlike any other eating place: a sensation of nervous agitation based on a necessity to rush even when you are not in a hurry, the urge to get back on the road when you and your machine have filled up and drained down, emanates from over the stylized eatery. There, alimentation and elimination vie for attention. Generally before fooding rites even start, everyone makes a general rush for the toilets, a mandatory first step in the preset course of events. Towards the end, at the checkout register, a small collection of cheap candies along with Tums for the Tummy is offered, as if the final stage in the process is eating a sweet and then a digestive, sometimes compacted into one single circular tablet. The main point here continues to be that when impartially computed, a significant, even remarkable, portion of each day is occupied with food-related activities.

We live in a society that tends to eat virtually all the time, without respect for the three squares of old. Consider coffee breaks and the snacking while walking or watching a film or TV. When the moments we eat candy or chewed gum are added up, the total of each waking day devoted to food mounts ominously; furthermore, with the inclusion of beverages, the sum is still heftier. Unlike our uncivilized ancestors, we eat and drink constantly, rarely from hunger or thirst.

An examination of the conditions in which food is devoured reveals a tendency towards asocialization, despite the occasionally more joyous social aspects. Fooding activities, manifested either by eating alone or within an environment in most modern contexts inhibit social intercourse. The effect of this situation must be appreciated not merely in terms of the actual intake of food but as part of the pattern of modern life and the capacity to relate to the natural world. For many city dwellers, the all-too-frequent activity of eating alone is degrading. Seated unceremoniously at counters in lunch rooms, diners, and delis, locked onto circular metal, leatherette- covered seats that rigidly snap into place facing an ugly mirror, or at fast-food outlets with encrusted glass, any attempt at establishing a human exchange while served the off-white, stool-like mashed potatoes in off-white Styrofoam containers with plastic utensils is effectively annihilated by harsh music and general clatter.

Another influential area for meal taking is readily forgotten, since it is absolutely inconsequential: lunches, dinners, and snacks served on airlines—millions daily—in which everyone is seated facing in the same direction, with the back of an unknown someone's head as the principal object of vision or someone alongside who you cannot even see for company. The fare is too familiar to describe, but the point to emphasize is that the actual eating occurs without looking at anyone in the eyes. The food itself resembles, but is a tiny bit superior to, hospital fare, which defines yet anothr locus for eating, in which the underlying principle is the TV frozen dinner conceived for an isolated individual.

Other popular outlet that offers alternatives to restaurants are pushcarts and food wagons located strategically throughout the central city. They hawk shish kebab, hot all-beef franks with overboiled colorless kraut, tacos as well as other pseudo-ethnic preparations among the fumes and dirt of the streets. These freshly prepared items appeal to mid-town secretaries and other moderately salaried employees who descend forty or fifty stories in jam-packed, high speed skyscraper elevators at 12 noon on the dot. A rewarding aspect of eating off stands is that one develops favorites and even establishes a rapport with the food provider. When weather permits, the luckier customers find unofficial, makeshift seating, perhaps on a low concrete wall; however, usually they stand alone or with an office mate after politely waiting on an orderly line for their turn to purchase the modest repast.

Reflecting newer trends, a proliferation of health-oriented vendors dispensing nuts (though high in cholesterol), and dried fruit or obscenely opulent looking, not to say oversize, fresh produce, tasteless shiny deep toned Delicious or Ida Reds that look more like plastic counterfeit clones than the real thing. Here, too, the mode of consumption remains fundamentally isolated: furtive, nervous, without human exchange, ritual or joy.

In what at first thought might seem the opposite, the luncheon experience, eating at two- and three-star, nominally French, Italian, or Japanese restaurants, executives, entrepreneurs, stock market and junk bond salespersons, or lawyers hosting their clients, hardly provides a homey, social happening. Tiny portions of overpriced, chicly undercooked *al dente* pasta in unacceptable, fundamentally un-Italian cream sauces, expensive but not especially fine wines and San Pellegrino mineral water are consumed in an overcrowded, noisy, contemporary Mafia-style ambiance. The art collector, of course, is likely to partake of his overly fresh and already soggy prosciutto and melon or raw fish lunch in a similar atmosphere with an associate or two paid for by the "firm" which, everyone understands, means the U.S. Government.

In the context of alternatives McDonald's and Burger King need not be singled out for special, high-minded criticism, easy as it might be to do so. To find their outlets in virtually every mid-size city in Germany seems incongruous; one was supposed to be constructed directly off the Piazza del Duomo in Florence to match an affiliate alongside the Spanish Steps in Rome. Yet, they have come to constitute a positive factor in smaller communities in rural America where the option in the past was a greasy EAT truck pit stop on a lonely interstate highway.

At least the chains, which tend to remain open in the wee hours, are bright, clean, have functioning rest rooms and allow their customers to linger. And they are cheap, certainly in comparison to full-scale restaurants, even diners. In fact, over the past few decades these fast food outlets have become acceptable meeting places for young people since they offer an element of supervision to parents, anxiously watching late, late TV until the precious offspring return home. Furthermore they employ a lot of the same kids who are the customers in a happy family atmosphere.

In addition to the actual serving and eating of food, leaving aside the gigantic edifice of the production process from farm to factory, is the network of related lucrative industries dealing with the body which, in turn, reveals the consequences of too much, the wrong kind, or too little food. More than a generation ago, perhaps two, a book unforgettably titled *You Are What You Eat*, seems to have been on the right track. These situations of body treatment will be examined shortly; at this juncture it is essential to appreciate the all-embracing impact of fooding which, I contend, can serve as a useful entry into the world of contemporary art, its making, packaging, distribution, and appreciation. Ancient adventures of food gathering are etched upon the collective memory of the race's battle for survival. In historic times, food consumption achieved a ritual status connected with pleasure and familial interrelations that finally came to involve selection and rejection, or simply put, matters of taste, with all the implicitly calibrated alternatives, some acquired, others inherited at the dinner table or at Mom's formica kitchen counter.

Within the catalogue of human experience, the structures surrounding food may be productively considered a testing ground for theories concerning the society as a whole, its cultural manifestations, modes of action, and more directly to the issues considered here, the processes of reception. To reiterate the crucial jump: similar observations and conclusions may be applied to the production and perception of recent art that was created under identical contextual conditions. Furthermore, aberrations associated with eating may be appropriated as analogous signs of excess within the art culture.

Beverages

In the United States, the consumption of imported wines at dinner, which saw an explosive increase after the end of the World War II, coincided with new events in American art. While one could write off as coincidence any correlation between the two events, wine collecting may provide material for a rewarding mini-study in measuring perception on a relatively selective, esoteric and specialistic level. In the more distant past, dry wine was largely shunned in America where drinking the sweeter varieties, Port, Sherry, Muscatel, were more popular, especially since their alcoholic content is higher, thus offering a quick and cheap high. To be sure, hip-pocket pints of Thunderbird and Night Train (with its famous image of a steam locomotive plunging through the void) are still the preferred beverage among city winos.

With new-found wealth, however, and perhaps reinforced by the experience of GIs stationed in Europe and mass tourism, traditional old world amenities were imitated, and with a vengeance. Even a semi-prestigious dinner party required serving at least an attentively chosen white and red, although rare is the individual who can convincingly distinguish a Barbera from a Barolo, not to mention a good from a slightly passed one or a bottle in which the odor of cork has altered the flavor of a Châteauneuf-du-Pape and is rejected, to the anxious waiter's chagrin, with a practiced flip of the wrist. In an analogous action, the advanced art gallery aficionado might dismiss a particular exhibition of a newcomer out of hand, no questions asked, and few have the confidence to challenge such authority. The appreciation of a bottle of dry wine is surely an attribute of cultivation representing gentility; on the snobbery scale it has to rank well above collecting 19th century postage stamps, perhaps on the level of amassing holograph letters of famous writers. That fine wines have become "collectibles" with a booming, and potentially busting, auction market in those very same houses that control the sales of old clocks, walking sticks, gems, and precious art is instructive, possibly a coincidence but one that should not go unnoticed, along with the fact that some of the same collectors specialize in several categories at once. Probably, too, in the case of the wine, the most rare and expensive examples are too old to be consumed, as fate would have it.

Still more recent in terms of attaining a substantial following is the custom of drinking imported mineral waters: Perrier with a slice of lime can legitimately be ordered at a fashionable cocktail lounge or hotel bar, although some impurities may have burst the Perrier artificial bubble, at least temporarily, as has been the case for San Pellegrino. In the past, mineral waters won their reputation for specific curative powers to dissolve stones, for instance, or as a digestion aid, to calm bilious livers, as a diuretic, a physic, and they were widely prescribed by physicians and still are. Michelangelo obtained relief from Acqua di Fuiggi, still distributed after four-hundred years and, naturally, available in the United States. On the other hand, as the regular public drinking water in Europe has become increasingly contaminated or at least ill-tasting, mineral water has evolved into a near necessity there, and seems progressively so in America for the same reasons. As with dinner wines, Americans must have learned about mineral water from trips abroad but its use has been successfully re-enforced by brilliant advertising and a new desire for presumed purity.

Households, even in the provinces, are stocked with Evian, Perrier, together with native sources from Maine to Oregon. The consumption of carbonated sodas, beer, wine coolers, has soared over the past few decades. Pampering of trivial whims that evolve from a constant need for fulfillment becomes in time the genesis of an absolute necessity. Skillful advertising has added notably to the demand and, in fact, to the entire process that it constantly stimulates. Considering the sheer billions spent on drinks of all kinds every year, the well-oiled, deeply professional advertising machinery made possible by the low cost of production has relevance within the context of modern reception and perception. Taste, need, style and peer acceptability are efficiently manipulated and countermanipulated, and one has to wonder whether similar or analogous occurrences, though presumably with greater refinement, are not found in the area of the fine arts, given the very nature of the media.

Corporations have deemed it desirable in terms of their public image and for marketing reasons to sponsor cultural activities, the way the beer industry has been the principal sponsors of broadcasting on radio and television sporting events. They have become indispensable for the operation of both professional and college sports; cultural institutions and performances are equally dependent upon industrial and private donors. Educational television would fold immediately without corporate sponsorship. The names, slogans, and what should be thought of as low-keyed tasteful public service-oriented advertisements are now actually the rule, not the shocking exception in the public "educational" media. Art museums are deeply dependent upon similar sponsorship. Paid out of public relations budgets, the sponsor expects and presumably earns a *quid pro quo*. If a costly exhibition of a Baroque painter is sponsored by a cigarette corporation, obviously the CEO assumes that the image value is worth the expense.

In a relatively new area in the cultural province, public or private foundations together with international corporations have turned to artistic restorations as a desirable area for their charitable contributions, since it promises to gild their public reputation. They are able to secure for their company or bank an endorsement from Masaccio or Rubens by paying for a restorative campaign, the wild card being the real or assumed need in the first place.

The unbridled consumption of beverages has stimulated pronounced secondary effects. In the case of wine and beer, as well as the yet to be discussed intake of hard liquor, all of which constitute part of the fooding mechanism, excessive consumption has led to severe illness and death. Alcoholism, which affects both sexes and all age levels, continues to be one of the most costly and psychologically harmful byproducts of drinking. It is enough to recognized the number of words that revolve around the subject in American English to be alerted to the depth that drinking has had on American life. Words like "inebriated, drunk, bombed, crocked, loaded, high, intoxicated, looped"—they never seem to end- are an indication of the problem, one I do not plan to explore here, although undoubtedly connections with food and perception are self-evident. Alcoholism does not appear to be as exclusively associated with contemporary life any more than does the misuse of food. Yet, its incidence among teenagers, for examples, signifies a new and certainly unwanted aspect of the post-war generation. Alcoholic beverages of the kind listed above are also a source for caloric intake, consequently occupying a part in the vicious cycle of obesity and related food disorders.

In recognition of the fattening effects of traditional beverages, colas and the like, the industry countered by using artificial, low calorie sweeteners, despite the fact that the long-term effects upon the human system of these chemicals are anything but reassuring. More recently the public has been offered "lite" beers and other drinks with reduced calories, though empirically there seems to be not a single beer belly the less. More than anything else, light cigarettes as with the "lite" beer are simply palliatives designed to soothe the conscience of the troubled purchaser. Reports indicate that with such new products, because of requirements for the kick, the consumer merely uses more than before and the final countdown is that as much of the unwanted element, calories or nicotine, is taken in as with the regular versions.

What emerges with raw clarity is a truly baffling situation in the more basic aspects of modern urban living, beginning with food consumption patterns, where the individual is faced with a constantly befuddling set of contradictory circumstances. An anarchic hierarchy of quality and alternative courses of action model the daily experience. The common routine related to the public aspects of city life and its visual environment serve to highlight this set of bewildering conditions, where the contours between the real, the apparent real and the fable are extremely fuzzy, rapidly and pitilessly faded in and out in a ceaseless flux. If the art of the generation spanning the 1960s—1980s has identical qualities, it is hardly any wonder. Yet the role of the art is more complex than merely mirroring its context, for in practice, especially as a result of the efficiency of the modern mass media, art went a long way towards shaping these very conditions, emphasizing and redefining them.

Chapter IV.
Eating Disorders and Contemporary Vision

The preoccupation with food, including the actual and psychological time and energy expended, has achieved the status of a national, if not world, epidemic, in the industrialized countries. Since intrinsic aspects of survival in conjunction with perception on basic levels, together with fundamental assumptions regarding style, are involved, the mechanisms surrounding food can provide a yardstick for measuring the society, patterns of reacting, preoccupations, sources of creativity and, especially for my argument, the context for its art.

One hardly needs to be reminded that food has been a bonafide subject matter for painters over the centuries. Persuasive pictorial innovations that have pointed to the most advanced modern expression were derived from Cézanne's rotting apples and Van Gogh's stoical, colorless consumers of potatoes. Eatables, eating utensils, and the planting, cultivation and harvesting as well as the sale of food have been painted by artists since the Renaissance. Having had its ups and downs, the subject saw a renaissance in the late 1950s and 1960s, the most prominent examples having been produced by Warhol, Wesselman, Thiebaud and Johns, and in three overblown dimensions by, among others, Oldenburg, which at the least constitute brilliant social commentary. Their revival of a privileged subject matter in art should be comprehended as a signal of the extent to which food-related concerns had permeated the social fabric. Campbell Soup cans, pastel pie slices, still life objects representing eatables, giant plastic hamburgers covered with a shiny plastic ketchup, finely wrought beer cans, actual pieces of fruit, caught the imagination of the generation along with depicting lunch rooms, Pizza Huts, and metallic diners.

Consider the ubiquitous, red and white labeled soup can with its endless implications for modern life. The success of an application in "high" art, in and of itself, is an indicator of magnetism of the subject. Canned foods have a century-old history and more, and can claim to be among the first of the "fast foods," as a product that with the expenditure of a few moments of preparation can be eaten: simply add water, heat, stir and *voilà*. The resulting standardized, impersonal, one may even say, multiple, fluid has the same flavor, consistency, smell and appearance at each of its millions and millions of applications every time, whether served in Chicago, High Falls, Southampton or Iowa City. The brew represents part of the "egalitarianization" of eating patterns in an America and beyond to be sure, that is distinguished by an unrivaled ethnic diversity. The can, including the wide-mouthed coffee tin, also had and continues to have a direct application by artists who tend to store their brushes in such convenient and cheap vessels. In that context, too, the coffee can evolved into the subject of artistic representations, with obvious autobiographical implications. This is not so much art for art's sake as art about art or, rather, about the act and fact of making art, which is surely one of the most persistent iconographies we have experienced in the past century. Furthermore, the coffee it once contained, Savarin or another formula, is a whole discourse of its own.

Artists, like handymen in their garages, deploy rinsed soup cans as containers to mix colors, to accommodate synthetic turpentine, blend varnish or to deposit cigarette butts. As one of the more common objects in our society, empty or full, they embrace an extensive spectrum of meanings to almost everyone, and hence it was a remarkable insight to artfully manipulate the potentialities of such a familiar into an unfamiliar configuration. Through expansion, multiplication, fragmentation, and color displacement, the object became a symbol, a flag, if you will.

Likewise, the all-American hamburger, despite its name, has import for everyone—an unpredictable universality rivaled only by Coke. Billions of them have been sold by one Macompany alone, and the numbers soar daily. Families from all regions of the country and every economic bracket serve the circular, flattened patty of ground beef in the identical manner: between halves of a tasteless spongy bun smothered with toppings. Within the fixed boundaries of its cylindrical essence, plenty of room is left for individualization: some opt for an inexplicable combination of mustard with spicy tomato ketchup, many add India relish alone or with a circle-within-a-circle Bermuda onion slice, others prefer lettuce and tomato with a lick of mayo as if it were a BLT, while traditionalists might prefer a slice of sour pickle chip. Fried or broiled on a grill, the burger can be eaten rare, medium-rare or well-done, and is traditionally accompanied by French fries. Hamburger preparation on the barbecue grill at home is a family theme with endless variations, in which the personality of the craftsman comes through even before the first bite. Within the limited boundaries imposed by custom, the creator enters the equation with all his expressive baggage and originality.

Canned foods, frozen food and especially the subcategory of single-portion, full-meal platters, the notorious TV dinner, have displaced cookery from the family kitchen, where improvisation and personalized expressionism reign, to factories in Long Island City. The standardized, flawless Campbell's Soup is never like its homemade ethnic prototype, prepared on the top of a stove, having a distinctiveness, both suffering and benefiting from the humors of the cook and the seasons of the year. In contrast, the commercial product is boiled in cavernous caldrons, flavored on the basis of market testing with plenty of salt and herbs to appeal to a mythical average. The final stirrings are provided by a giant mechanical shovel immediately before the orangy-red, translucent liquid is poured in endless rows into the separate cans. After a few decades, the canned product actually transformed itself in the collective memory of the commonwealth from an anonymous, androgynous concoction into the soup mother used to make. In a Pavlovian overturning, canned soup exudes an aura of nostalgia for the good old days when the family ate their delicious piping hot soup, probably the most inexpensive item one could buy, with Sunshine's Krispy Saltines in the kitchen while watching Jackie Gleason. Precisely this kind of transformation or displacement was made vivid to me years ago when a shoe buyer from Bellevue Ohio who was assigned to Florence (not Ohio which must have one, but Italy) for a five year stretch confided that what he missed most from the States was the delicious Franco-American brand canned gravy he ate over a couple of slices of soggy Wonder Bread two or three times a week. A lesson is floating here somewhere on the viscous surface: our habits and our taste are readily conditioned and once they take root are nigh impossible to dislodge even with *funghi porcini* from the Aosta Valley.

Contemporary prints and print collecting

Soup in a can represents a simple, mass-produced, mass-distributed, mass-media-advertised and mass-consumed product dispersed in an intrinsic shape, the segment of a cylinder, which supports the Parthenon and if you take off its paper jacket, it appears to be a piston that powers a Boeing 747. Coincidentally (but are there really ever any?) some of the images of the soup cans were conducted in graphic media, that is, in multicopy runs. The relationship is worth pursuing: prepared in silk screens, lithographs and mixed-media graphics, the images of cans, a most common and intrinsically worthless objects in society, in singles or in multiples, command incredible prices (naturally, only for those by artists who have achieved an international reputation). Hence the counterfeit of a common, mass-produced, worthless object also produced in multiples becomes a highly prized object.

To further complicate the matter, these concoctions are not necessarily or even commonly cooked up by the artists themselves. For the most part, as painters they are not especially proficient nor specifically trained in graphic media, a branch of art that conventionally requires years of experience. Rather, they are

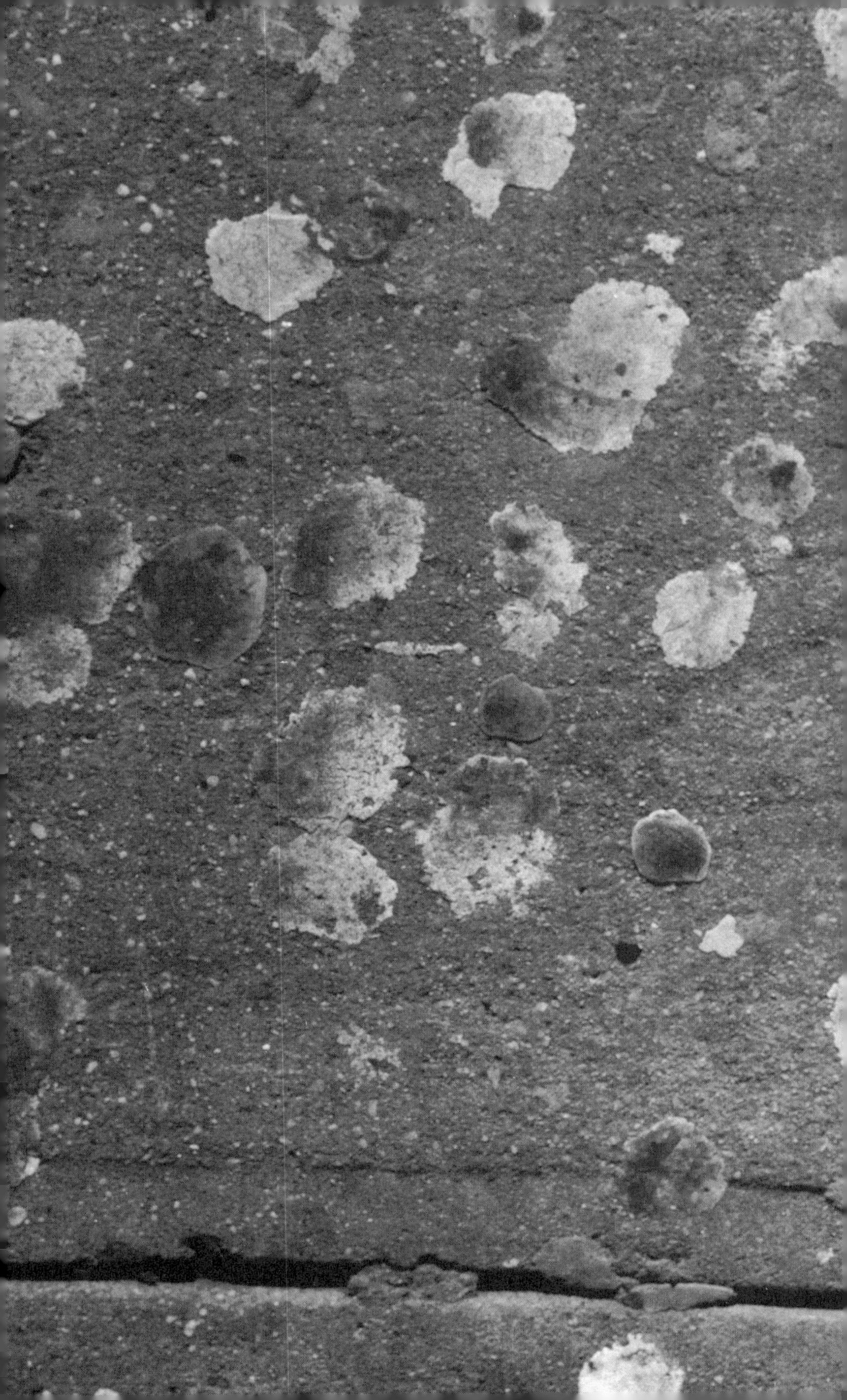

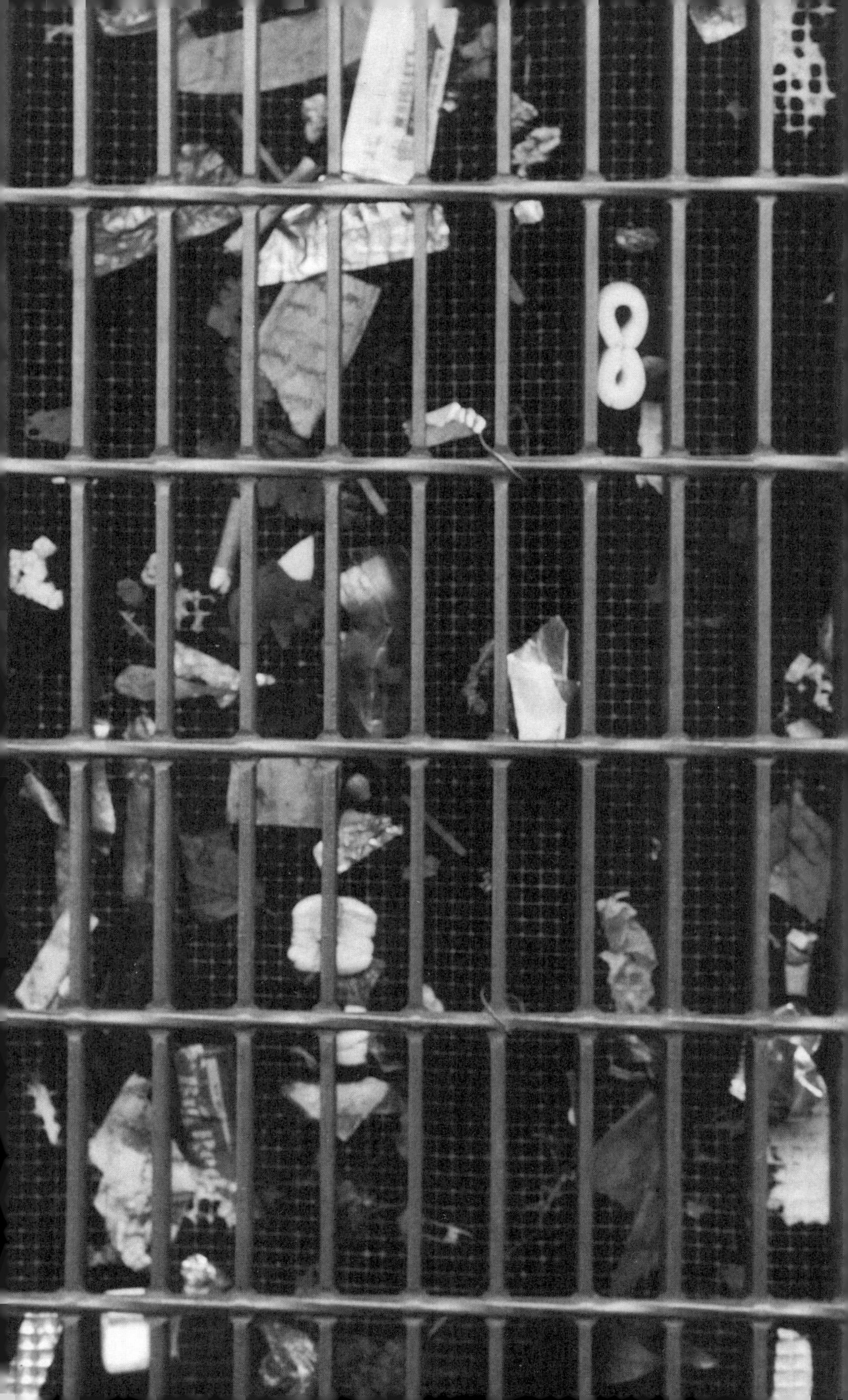

prone to pass on to an assistant skilled in such matters or to an artisan, perhaps a star graduate of Wroclaw Academy, Poland, a drawing, sketch, or watercolor notation that is then worked up for the process. Alternatively one of their paintings, sometimes itself derived from printing or from photographic models, is transferred by professionals, occasionally under the direction of the busy, big-name artist holding his cellular phone, but more often without much interaction. What results is a run of a hundred or more so-called "originals," plus unnumbered runs of artist's proofs. All are presumably hand-signed by the artist, though even at this stage one cannot be certain. We know of an example in which the artist's mother lovingly did the autographing. The final products are prized by an avid and gullible collecting public, often those collectors of old wines or Napoleonic gold coins, and find their way to prestigious museum graphic collections. These prints, I suggest, have only the remotest relationship to the artist credited with their creation. Sold to a fairly unsophisticated array of contemporary print collectors, with claims of originality, they are really an outgrowth of either a tongue-in-cheek or cynical manufacturing system, no more than a Toshiba assembly line.

The market value of a fairly simple preparatory sketch in the process I have enumerated or in a variation is swollen 100 or 1000 fold; the totals become staggering, essentially for the single drawing. If, that is, a drawing by a big-name artist can command, say, 15,000 dollars, the edition of the print runs into the millions. Not even the most overpriced surgeon, criminal lawyer or home run king could hope to approach the hourly intake. The pricing of these prints, especially those produced in the past 30 years, is a configuration parallel to rare postage stamps, usually called "classics," in which auction houses have the prominent role. An elaborate system of grading has been invented, with an infinity of nuances depending on the numbers in the sequence, whether one has a set or not, the quality of the particular print, the complexity, the condition, and so on, all of which tend to bolster the rarity of the object and consequently the evaluations. At the summit of the paper mountain, the highest ranking sheets are monotypes. As with all collectibles, however, the bottom line is a function of the supply and the demand. Yet, in the case of the prints, and quite possibly stamps and coins as well, an element of manipulation, as with Wall Street's junk bonds, lurks behind the tenuous market.

In distinction to the multiples of mainly decorative prints, the value of an original drawing by the same artists may be held to be far less valuable, although a drawing is an entirely unique object without repetitions. One might even go so far as to conclude that the mechanical copy of an object in our society has become more precious than a unique one, perhaps because the collector feels more confident when there are others in the same boat; the risk of appearing foolish is heavily reduced. The validation for a taste and a willingness to pay for those flags come in quantity. One person can be wrong, but can twenty leading collectors, backed up by a half-dozen leading curators from a handful of America's finest museums, and with critical acclaim the art press?

The fake

Falsification and the prodigious activity that surrounds imitation is a related phenomenon to the "semi-original" print, though perhaps a step lower on the ethical ladder. Every age had its falsifiers and ours has its share, often in the area of prints. The "classics" like Mirò and Picasso in particular have served as a lucrative rock candy mountain since their prints appeal in particular to relatively unsophisticated buyers who are attracted by brand names, the top of the line, the Jaguar. Since an active market for more recent prints has been tuned, forgeries of these objects have found their way into the marketplace, mainly because the techniques and processes of their production are ambiguous in the first instance and because the dealers and collectors are themselves relatively ill-equipped to distinguish the good, that is original, from the fake.

The fascination with fake masterpieces in painting is definitely on the rise, and here a distinction should be quickly drawn between devoted copies of museum masterpieces and true deceptions. There is a thriving market for announced self-proclaimed fakes, Cézannes and Van Goghs by the score, for example, but any other artist can be duplicated, depending purely on demand. They are offered at a tiny fraction of the price of an original and at worst have conversational appeal. Such a work offers, in distinction to a good reproduction, a handmade object, one that can even increase in value, often an indispensable ingredient in more recent collecting, and has the feel of an original. Exhibitions of fakes and forgeries from every period have fascinated an enthusiastic public. In the category of the sophisticated fakes made as a genre to be palmed off as the original, undoubtedly engender amazement for the pure skill manifested. Satisfaction, too, is derived from the recognition that art experts and acclaimed museum experts can and have been taken in, sometimes to the tune of millions of dollars and with egg yolk on their bow ties. At the same time, high quality fakes challenge our evaluations of art as a whole and the periods from which the forgeries originated. When, for example, a painting is adjudged an original Vermeer its value would be in the millions of dollars; if it is by the famous forger of the 1930s, Van Meergren, who was able to fool distinguished experts and a famous Nazi collector, it may be worth relatively little, although the admitted forgeries by the frustrated Dutch modernist painter have increased in value more recently, partly because of the notoriety that his fakes have achieved.

Certainly, as all art scholars are aware, diverse old masters fakes inhabit the world's major museums and still others are found on the walls of provincial museums. In the past, the American tax structure abetted the donation of art works to public institutions, including colleges and universities; their monetary evaluations and thus the tax deduction were based upon attributions of sometimes self-styled experts and were inevitably inflated. Shop versions, replicas, old copies and even outright fakes ornament ivy encrusted buildings of leading universities, which are a frequent and fairly unsophisticated recipient of this category of generosity. Private collections have their share of outright fakes, sometimes with the dealer's knowledge, we must assume, and sometimes not.

Every generation or so a team of experts seems determined to embarrass the art world with prominent reports about a favorite Rembrandt, like the *Polish Rider* in the Frick Collection, which we are authoritatively assured is neither Polish nor painted by Rembrandt. If we are to believe the Rembrandt specialists now in vogue, the widely reproduced and much adored painting was actually painted by a weak follower of the master. In this issue of attributionism, which should not be confused with the questions surrounding fakes, one must commend the earnestness of these experts, and they may even prove to be correct, although I for one suspect that it is far too soon to make the final call (and for the record, I prefer to consider the *Polish Rider* as by Rembrandt). The effect upon the wider, non-trained public unaware of the rise and fall of fashions even in connoisseurship, has to be upsetting. The result opens the distinct possibility that in art, one guess is as good as another. There are, at the least, vast areas of uncertainty, even about the most sacred of cows.

Renaissance and modern forgeries of ancient Greek and Roman statuary are well-documented, and even Michelangelo was accused of producing such a statue as a young sculptor. In our own confident times, fakes have fooled trained authorities of major museums who purchased antiquities of controversial authenticity and fictional provenances, including more than one Etruscan "masterpiece." Lawsuits and countersuits are tracked with general enchantment and even glee, notably when it becomes known that pompous bearded professorial types who speak with exaggerated English accents despite their Midwest origins, have been duped. The recent case with Modigliani, an impressive number of whose paintings have been forged over the past half century, is illustrative. Several students from the local academy of art in his native Livorno, for their own amusement, as students might do anywhere, faked or at least trumped up a few sculptures that could be taken as originals by the artist, who sculpted, especially as a young man. After the blocks were cut with a Black and Decker chain saw, the story goes, they were thrown into a ditch and fished out sometime later, only to be "discovered" with fanfare. Several world-class experts, following the stamp of approval as to the authenticity of the discoveries by the leading local fine art official in the region, gravely announced, with typical pomp and circumstance, the importance of the new finds, including brilliantly honed, novel critical insights. To err is human, but the incident underscores the treacherous state of the authentication system and must have been yet another blow to everyone's self confidence when it comes to art. Similar recent episodes have surfaced when a purported Michelangelo study, a gesso model for the *David* and a "new" Donatello relief of the *Madonna and Child*, coincidentally turned up in time for a celebratory exhibition of the artists' works. Both are surely modern objects.

Fakes and forgeries are also widespread in the domain of non-Western art, in particular for Pre-Colombian sculpture. Certainly, the effect of this large operation is to undermine the already shaky self-confidence of not only the general public but collectors and museum curators and members of eminent boards of trustees. And despite the introduction of fairly sophisticated devices and techniques, the final judgment is often pure connoisseurship. When scholars openly dispute the claims of one another, for example, in the case of a valuable French Baroque picture by Georges de la Tour in the Metropolitan Museum of Art, the public is completely at sea. More complicating still is the fact that one of the strongest defenders of the authenticity of the picture, a knighted English art historian, was himself a famous fake — a Soviet agent for decades in the heart of London society.

Along with the art, the public is battered with a vast array of fake and near-fake products, especially but not exclusively in the line of food. Margarine, first concocted as a cheap butter substitute which was first white in color, if memory holds, can be classified in the same category as the canned tomato soup that mother used to heat up. Think back to those charred English muffins smothered with "butter" which was of course spreadable margarine, and deep translucent violet Concord grape jelly, another all-American favorite, relatively unknown elsewhere. Sugar substitutes are used more commonly than the real thing, which of course has not been the real thing for decades, anyway. We have meat derived of soy flour, artificial maple syrup formulated from God knows what, and veal cutlets which are actually breast of turkey. Salt has become a definite no-no, so that false salt has been introduced.

The all-embracing appearance of artificial substitutes is an accepted facet of modern life, and does not really trouble many people anymore. The Japanese small car was a perfect example, in a process where the imitation becomes the real thing, the model to be copied by others. My point here is that we are used to fakes, forgeries, substitutes, replacements, derivations and are entirely untroubled by the fact of non-originality. Naturally this same attitude has entered into the arts; indeed, how could it be otherwise?

Food and Modern Art

As part of a discourse on the context of contemporary art, I have been advocating right along that a relation to food can be readily sketched. Two principal considerations may be drafted: (1) food products represent a vital aspect of the consumer society, and the surrounding machinery is inseparably tied to all other aspects of modern life, including and especially those connected with visual experience; and (2) the prodigious universe related to food involves fundamental issues of style, rarity, and the habits of taste that are regularly created, diffused and undone through skillful manipulation.

Scanning the cast that might be observed at a typical shopping mall in up-state New York or in Terre Haute, Indiana *tout de suite* discloses the extent of the fooding phenomenon. The conditions in New York City are slightly different, possibly because of the extensive number of foreigners who reside there, or because city life is disparate enough to generate a distinctive physical appearance among its inhabitants, like Parisians from the rest of the French; surely they reveal a different gait, another pace and mode of dress. Among the most striking presences of the human landscape outside the city are obese young people in impressive numbers, although the share of overweight middle-aged and older people is not to be dismissed easily either. Though the observation is entirely without scientific or statistical foundation, fat people in the suburbs and especially in the outlying localities stand out more than their big city counterparts. One notices in particular those married couples where both young husband and wife are hand-holding jumbos, as much as double their adolescent weight by the time they reach their mid-twenties, with one or two fat-cheeked, pants-busting toddlers in tow. It is sufficient to follow them on their shopping forays through the wide aisles of the supermarket, in distinction to the crowded narrow ones at the University Market, to understand their eating habits which dictate their physical appearance.

One might well start with the shopping cart itself, which has expanded in size more recently as buying patterns have, so that one can now put into its wire hull, not dissimilar structurally to the refuse container in the city, a massive quantity of found objects, a 24-can case of Coke, 10-pound sacks of frozen French Fries, giant size packages of Pampers and economy 12-packs of super soft and fluffy toilet rolls. And sitting like an infant prince of Spain, bare fat legs sticking out of the specially designed openings, is the child, dressed in clothes whose material comes from petroleum byproducts giving irrevocable commands. This is the performance of shopping for the orientation of the industrialized world's children. In the long term an experience repeated thousands of times cannot fail to have had an indelible imprint, specifically upon eating patterns. The patterns of selection from a variety of options as the little fellow reaches maturity, and who knows, in his pattern of looking at art in museums and galleries and finally in the actual purchasing of one of those prints of a bottle of Coke or a reproduction of it, have been deep-frozen into place.

For the past couple of generations, from a very early age we have been exposed to a never-ending multiplication of shelves filled with brightly colored objects that vie with each other for our attention. Packaging is a determining factor in the universe of the food industry, for it does not merely establish an image that becomes intimately associated with the product and the brand, but shares a vocabulary with "high" (which to many of us means "real") art. The creation of recognizable logos or the design of the lettering on a Kellogg's box, for example, has become a center of concentration within the advertising constellation. Not surprisingly, many painters who have attained prominence in the generation that has just ended were keenly aware of the impact of such mainly graphic imagery, including, not incidentally, the green ink engravings that are used to pay for the purchases. The notion of idealizing or at least monumentalizing money in the first place, and the ready reception and curiosity on the part of the art public, exposes much about the period and its modes of expression and ingrained habits. By the end of the 1980s, cash money was all but a secondary mode of payment and instead of showing off with a wad of twenties, the wealthy and the would-be wealthy flaunt a stack of credit cards.

The Kellogg's Corn Flakes boxes and the Campbell's Soup cans invite a sociological reading whose interpretations are rich in potentialities for the society. The point is that the vitaminized and mineralized child almost from the beginning of life is accustomed to seeing an array of objects, in different minimally repeated sizes and shapes with alternating designs, patterns and logos printed on them, which offer a visual engagement as well as signifying something else, namely, the food (or other objects, like Brillo or sanitary pads or dry dog bones composed of wheat flour, if the mutt is really lucky) inside. Moving down the aisles the arrogant heir-apparent to the mortgage and the car payments promptly learns which of the colorful packages he wants and, make no mistake about it, which ones he does not want, commanding Mommy or Daddy what to buy. It is mainly a Yes or No configuration, an On and Off situation, so that the presentation can be familiar, consoling, and even mouthwatering.

In all fairness, this kind of experience is hardly new, having unfolded for millennia, at the town market, in the oasis, in village fairs. In many parts of the world, open markets are still preferred when a choice is available, and surely with reason. In the market, one deals with independent operators who over time establish a rapport with their clients. The seller of fruits and vegetables watches the child grow, calls him by name, pays appropriate compliments, presents him or her with a greengage plum in season. In other words, a one-to-one exchange was superseded in most supermarkets where the entire act of selecting has been impersonalized. No element of human salesmanship is involved; only the decoration on the box, the backup media advertising accumulated in the memory bank of the customers and naturally the price are determining factors, together with (relative) need. Of course, with these items, as with everything else including those ever-present and overpriced prints, *caveat emptor*. A three-quart container of liquid laundry detergent, with a homey, computer friendly, three-letter name, can cost substantially more than three times the amount of three one-quart ones, in a Trinitarian disruption of the expected.

The children of the past thirty or more years have had a constant and profound contact with television that has consisted of a militant barrage of food and beverage advertising. Thus, early on the child's tastes and desires have been exploited in a manipulation that finds confirmation in the direct confrontation with the product on the supermarket shelves and piled up on the corner of aisles. As they recognize the advertised objects in all their physical glory, the association with the music, the concentration-demanding cartoons and the enjoyable entertainment flip onto the back-lighted screen of the child's mind. Besides, familiarity as a factor in making the choice of product can be decisive, like seeing the real Mona Lisa in the Louvre.

When, precisely, did the preoccupation with food begin, one that set into motion excesses and accompanying eating disorders? The first events a baby in a well-to-do society is subjected to, and ones that are reinforced for at least the next ten or twelve years in a constantly increasing crescendo, are urgings to "eat, eat." By songs, ditties, little skits, games, cuddling, threats, or bribery, the mouths of the little ones are stuffed to capacity. Nothing generates greater happiness in the anxious mothers and fathers than having a child with a good appetite, and when absent, it is just cause for endless visits to the pediatrician, child psychologist and hand clasping by troubled grandparents. Part of the explanation is that generation of parents' children are approximately the same ages as the artists who dominated the 1960s, 1970s and 1980s. The establishment art leaders were often either the children or grandchildren of mostly poor, ill-fed immigrants. Out of reaction to their own or at least hereditary past, we can suppose, the new mothers wanted their children to flourish and never be subject to the ugly pains of hunger. Furthermore, having abundant food for the children was a sign of getting out of the ghetto or the dismal sharecropping farm of southern Italy, Greece, Ireland or Alabama. While a fat youth may be socially unattractive, a skinny infant is an insult to the entire society as well as to the parents, and is a condition to be avoided at all costs, perhaps even more so among the poor than the rich.

Back a generation or two, down on the farm in southern Illinois or in the old country, and still today in most Third World situations, urging a kid to eat is out of the question. The real challenge is finding something to put in his mouth and sharing the little that is available with sisters and brothers. Food related abuses and diseases prevalent in advanced societies are hardly a problem for other places where there is not enough to eat. A devastating divergence has taken place between the enormous displacement of energies required in the primordial past for survival and modern food-gathering practice.

Recognizing the inherent desire of parents for their children to be well-fed, the colossal advertising machinery is cunningly aware of the baby market in developing product recognition and purchases. The extensive choices of flavors of baby foods available in jars which have dominated for at least two generations are exceptional, far beyond those that were available hardly a century ago. Mothers (especially mothers, but fathers, too, have had and continue to have a role) quickly begin to learn what the child seems to prefer, and what he will eat with gusto, and what he does not like and what he rejects. The child might just love that thick mush that in children's food language is known as chicken soup, although there is not much chicken and it is not really soup. The baby foods imitated the traditional strained fare that mothers prepared daily, usually composed of a vegetable compound plus a bit of ground meat, all passed through a strainer. Choices were virtually nonexistent, in contrast to today's endless options in baby food, flavors of natural teas, or pet foods for that matter. As for the latter, we know that they are meant to please the pet's owners and not the cats and dogs who hardly notice the difference between a fish-flavored and a meat-flavored meal. While we now have vitamin-enriched animal foods to follow that of baby foods, I wonder whether it is not time to reduce the salt content for the beloved hounds and felines, following the common understanding that too much salt could lead to a stroke or hardening of the arteries? Allegedly natural products have already entered the pet market, and some avant-garde concoctions blazon their box pridefully as having "no artificial color."

The Obese

The subject of the obese and of obesity should be considered when examining the tone of life in the nation, the image and self-image of its people, and of particular pertinence to the arguments taken in the present discussion: modes and aberrations of perception. Overweight and even severely overweight women often envisage themselves as sensually attractive and can be found wearing tight, revealing clothes that accentuate colossal behinds and cavernous bosoms. It is hardly unusual to find them in Big Mamma jeans and spiky high heels, their appearance enticingly augmented by heavy make-up and bizarre, attention-producing jewelry.

Despite the pervasive negative propaganda about excessive weight, obese women frequently consider themselves as desirable, as if living in a world of trick mirrors that cause them to appear far thinner than they really are. After all, virtually without exception images in the advertising repertoire show women not only as young but also lean and, depending upon a particular year or two, as thin as a twig. Hence, obese women seem to march or waddle countercurrent in the face of all the publicity, Hollywood and TV twiggy stars, fashion models, Miss Americas, and high school beauty queens, some of whom they were only a short few years and two babies before. One might even suggest that, in part at least, being fat is a rebellion and rejection of the conventional and imposed behavior: bumper stickers, a popular expressive outlet, reading "FAT IS BEAUTIFUL" or "FAT IS SEXY" are their battle cries, and why not?

Obese men tend to be prideful of their mountainous bellies, often overtly displayed by thick designer suspenders that function to enframe the protuberance longitudinally, and heavy upper arms equivalent to the thighs of an average person. At least in limited instances, especially among manual workers and professional football players, weight is conflated with strength, ability and manliness. These individuals customarily appear in beer commercials on television where their bulk is considered as advantageous. Contests in which the winner eats the most hamburgers or the most chili, or drinks the most cans of beer in the shortest time are popular events at state fairs and town parties. The obese man may dress with his brightly colored attention-commanding shirt left open to broadcast his impressive bulk. Presumably, like their mates, these men do not have a clear conception of their appearance, or at least the frame of their thinking runs contrary to norms. Sexism operates in this realm: for a man to be fat seems to be more acceptable socially than for a woman to be so.

The absolutely reverse situation occurs among anorexics, who even though they may be starvation thin, see themselves in the obverse of the fun house mirror, as fat, ugly and undesirable, a fearful reality. More about the anorexic will follow, but one should realize that we are dealing in extremes, the obese and the anorexic, very often with aberrations in perception. They are persons who have been subjugated to long periods of thought and visual manipulation that has affected their entire being. With the click of a mind set, the fat become thin, and the thin fat (and for that matter the old, young and the young, old). Where reality crops up is anyone's guess, and then is it real reality or the reality of fantasy, which may be still more real. How tall is tall in professional basketball, for instance? And what are the measures? It is getting taller all the time.

In this context, I am not thinking of representations of fat or thin people, *à la* Botero or Giacometti, or even Rubensians, which are either private stylistic options or appealing to patrons.

Television Viewing and Eating

Returning to the supermarket and our up-state obese couple holding hands as they pass down the aisles, the fountainhead of their excess weight becomes patent. Beverages constitute a profound part of their caloric intake: beer by the six-pack, if not the case, light or regular, it hardly matters when the quantities are substantial. The routine of sitting in front of the TV—to watch, typically, a sporting event with a couple of beers renewed at regular intervals and neatly coordinated with the commercial messages and urination—is a damaging pastime for a substantial portion of the population who have weight "problems," especially in the provinces.

Not unlike the situation of the child whose identification of products in the supermarket is linked with the image of the same product on the blinking screen, so his father and sometimes his mother too, passively sit actually drinking the same brand of beer that is being advertised in insistently pernicious, often witty spots. As an aside, one might wish to notice the pattern in which these advertisements are repeated, sometimes back to back, and at others with fixed rhythms, hammering home the message without pity.

The devotion to national sporting events is a feature of the culture that deserves reflection in the context of artistic creation in a modern society because of the appeal it has to nearly everyone. Artists are not immune to the pageantry and excitement of these spectacles—the Playoffs—in unending rounds in which the last two minutes last half an hour, the World Series, the Cotton, Sugar or Rosebowl, and the culmination: the Super Bowl. The system has become so thoroughly oriented to earnings and, consequently, to the entertainment content that traditional playing seasons no longer have any significance. Like fruits and vegetables that one used to eat only in their proper time, they are sold now all year round. One ends up watching hockey playoffs in the warmth of late spring, and finals of the professional basketball season, traditionally a winter sport, in the early summer. Football, in the past a fall game, now lasts throughout the winter. Cherries, reasonably tasteless at that, in November are the equivalent. In simple terms, the vast network of sporting events and the connected industries that surround them has exploited the activity to such an extent that in the past few decades the very meaning of sports has been turned upside down, like the canvasses of a well-regarded, but slightly passé though still youngish, contemporary German painter. The players constantly seem to grow taller, fatter, more grotesque and more removed from the physiques of the spectators. Here, as in so many aspects of modern life, the contours between the real and the unreal are obscured.

The star system reveals a close parallel between the art world and the modern sports industry. Thus, a super seven-footer for the Los Angeles Lakers may earn millions annually with multi-year contracts, or the home run slugger for the New York Yankees may achieve as much as 5 or 6 million dollars a year (Oh, for the days of King Kong Keller!). The situation is similar too for star painters, renowned representatives of the 1960s—1980s generation, whose works command prices that are not 10 times that of a pretty-good (reputation-wise, though not necessarily intrinsically) painter of proven achievement with scores of exhibitions on his *curriculum vitae*, not 100 times as much, but 10,000 times as much. The reasonably good basketball guard straight out of college who may have even been on a Big Ten championship team, and who has won prizes and trophies galore, usually cannot even make the bench of an NBA team. If he insists upon earning his living by his unique skill, he sometimes ends up playing abroad if he is lucky, as a professional in Israel, or

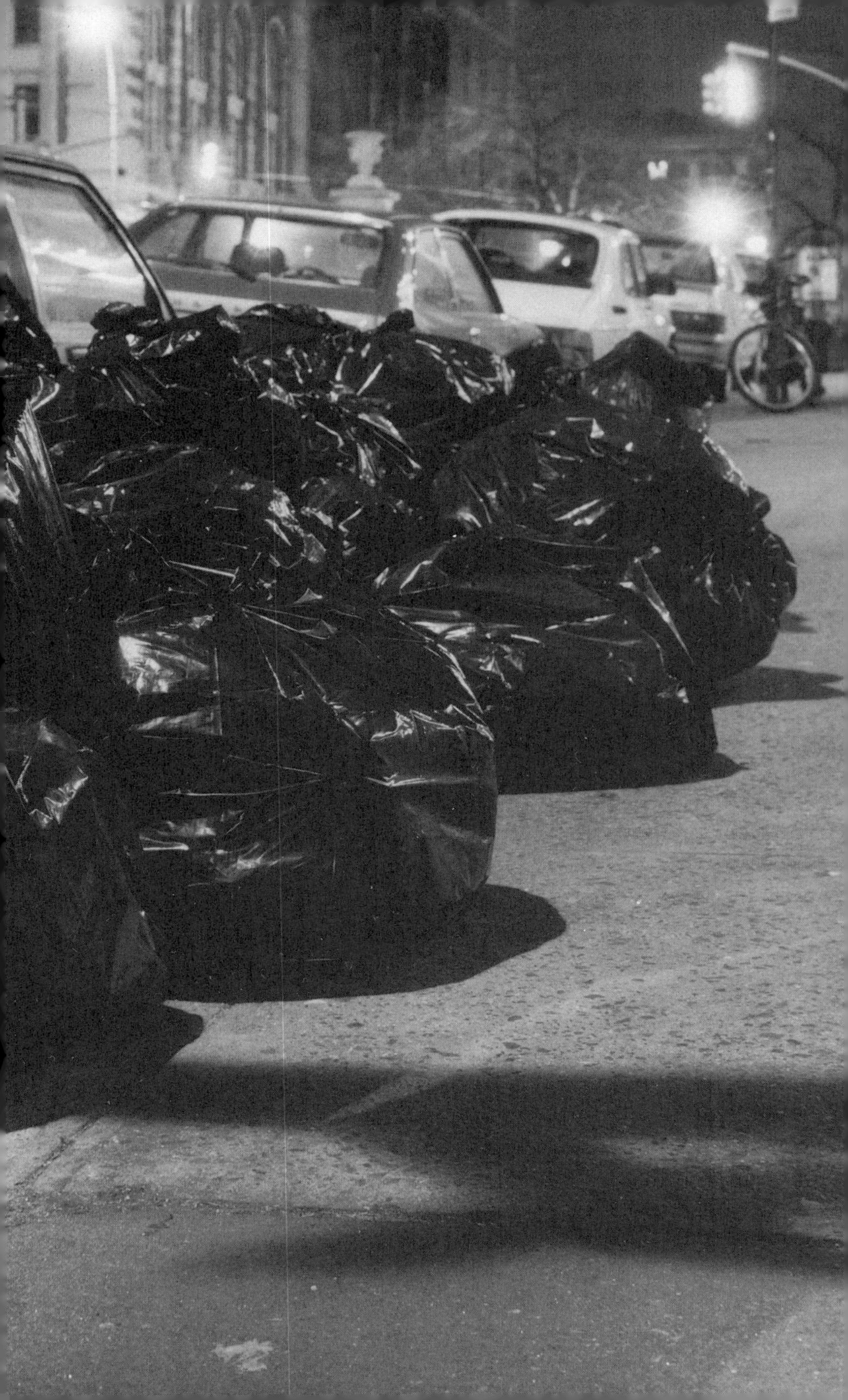

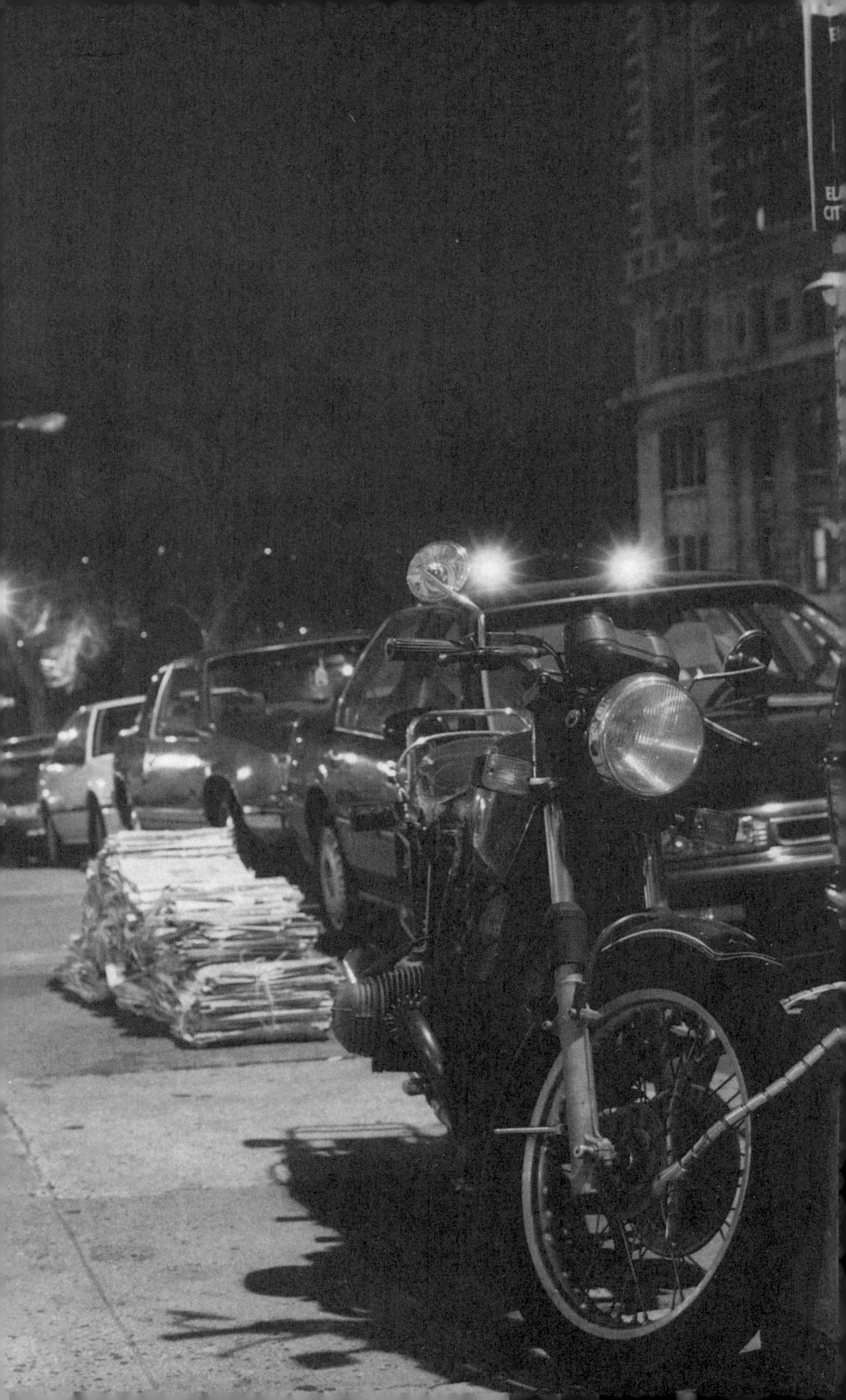

representing a milk company in Italy, or for a semi-pro club for a few hundred dollars a game back in the States. Women athletes, like women artists, have had an even more difficult, if not impossible, time. The kind of disequilibrium between establishment success and absence of success in the arts, while part of a paradigm, is degrading to the system, and even to those artists "on the top." Irrespective of morality, sincerity, and ability, a chasm has evolved between the highly successful and the everyday practicing artist who seeks virtually in vain to earn a living making art that has few parallels in the past and must be assigned to the effects of conditions dominated by an intricate schematization of the market.

Why adult men or women, choose to locate themselves in front of the flickering tube night, after night year after year may require an assortment of explanations, but the most convincing is the simple fact that television provides a cheap evening's distraction which, when spiked by a low-grade high, dulls the mind in preparation for a night's sleep. While drinking wine or something more alcoholic from the "package store" is possible, these are less common companions to TV spectatorship. In the country, or at least in provincial areas, the alternatives for spending an evening after work, especially in harsh weather, are considerably fewer than in the city. Unexpectedly, one tends to walk much more in the city, to survey the store windows and look at each other and away from each other more than in the suburbs or the country. It is the rare bird indeed who walks along country road instead of riding in his all-American Subaru pickup truck.

Added to the beer drinking while watching television is the widespread ingestion of carbonated soft drinks or insidiously sweetened fruit-flavored solutions for the kids that contain only a tiny percentage of fruit juice, the rest being dulcified water. Vitamin C which had been distilled from the juice in the first place has been added as a supplement. Coffee with milk or half and half and two sugars — bloating as well as fattening — are favored by some adults. Or milk shakes. Furthermore, if liquids were the only caloric intake involved with TV watching, the situation would be grave enough, but "goodies" inescapably go along with it, like rock-hard Pennsylvania Dutch pretzels, salted dry roasted nuts with a touch of paprika, spicy crackers, as well as more ambitious partners, like hero sandwiches. Thus, in the shopping session, these items and their components are musts on the list, filling the basket, layer by irregular layer.

Television viewing, like fooding to which it is closely interrelated, remains one of modern society's most routine experiences, repeated daily in an unremitting pattern, like the sections of the sidewalk in the city. Formerly located exclusively in the living room, sets are placed all over the house, from bedrooms to playrooms and probably no longer viewed much in the living room, as in the good old days when the average family had only one. The devices come in various sizes for various purposes, including tiny two-inch portables for those on the run, carried together with their beepers. Habits being what they are, housewives, children, and the elderly, especially when alone, have at least one set on all the time. Those who return home from work automatically click on a set, perhaps not watching with much concentration. Everywhere, in each room where people are confined, the monstrous slightly curved blinking eye is a presence. On its retina images frolic, but it also seems to have a reverse purpose: that of watching the viewer. All those menacing screens located in the open in every room in an apartment or in a house, and here we must include the computer, are not only stared at by the spectator but are themselves enormous eyes that intrude and spy upon the viewer as he picks his nose, sips his beer, munches the salty, deep-fried chips.

We should contemplate the mere act of viewing in its own right, in the setting of perception and reception, before considering actually what is to be viewed. Usually one is fairly immobile while watching and no doubt it is difficult to successfully engage in other activities simultaneously, like conversation, reading, or sexual intercourse. An insidious aspect of televiewing is that one tends to watch passively, frequently without deep interest in what is being offered, but however determined one may be not to look, the mechanism is such that it is impossible to entirely disengage. In a related mechanism, the routine of being entertained while eating one of the three squares, in distinction to snacking, has been the norm for decades for American children. Their parents inevitably have breakfast with the Morning News, there is usually a break at lunch which tends to be eaten out anyway, but again at dinner back with the tube and the fork.

The usual home setting has a television set on at all times, day and night, which constitutes another of those visual habits that should be taken as a given when considering modern reception and perception of art, and even the very production of it. The sheer number of hours involved is one steady factor. The second: as we have already seen, television produces images on a flat (or really slightly curved) two dimensional surface that has a frame and within that frame the images cavort. The presence of color, and color of a very special sort, expands the experience, perhaps making it ever more irresistible. Furthermore, some artists use video as a medium for their expression, blurring the distinction between art and non-art.

As is stressed in all discussions, television viewing places the spectator into a passive mode. Alternatively, creativity, sex, sports, seem to be more acceptable to watch than to actually participate in. Considering the popularity of soap operas: voyeurism has become the preferred non-activity. Actual physical participation seems the aberration. Certainly in a world of highly paid, skilled professionals, the chap with average skills, appearance, physical attributes and intelligence feels disadvantaged. The personalities on the screen are better looking, speak more skillfully, are more finely dressed and groomed, are evidently more successful sexually and financially. In other words, on infinite levels, television can be a debilitating and demeaning non-activity, affecting lives and choices more than anyone might wish to acknowledge. Additionally, the professional performers who are familiar have double realities: they *are* the characters they play in dramas and in variety shows, as they are also persons who have carefully monitored private lives. The fictive *persona* and the private *persona*, in an awkward and disjointed splicing of reality, are the subject of the envy and imagination of millions.

Art produced over the recent past must be approached with television as part of the cultural compound, just as linear perspective was in the fifteenth century. The arts have to compete for the public's attention with elaborate, brassy, heavily stylized and super-professionalized entertainment and maneuvered sporting events. Granted that the more sophisticated individuals in the society are less addicted to the television than the average, nonetheless few are entirely free of it, or of even greater importance, were free of it as children. Subtle Morandi bottles and Mondrian color blocks are not eye-stoppers, nor are the little Dutch Masters, the Spanish still life painters, Chardin, or the Sienese Sassetta. Caravaggio and the dramatic Baroque masters come closer to competing on common ground, while Renaissance sensibilities, like Botticelli, are too tame. We require an art that is capable of vying with other forms of entertainment. The more dramatic and absurd in the Dada sense the presentation, the better able to intrude upon the habits of the current culture: packaging the Pont Neuf, arranging neon lights to blink on and off in endless cycles, transforming the sacrosanct stars and strips into painted and graphic images, producing a plastic carrot the size of an apartment building or a Swiss Army Knife that could be used by Gulliver, such are startling enough to shake the attention of the viewer away from the tube, memories of the tube, or other competing forms of amusement.

Hence also the temptation to remake favorites, like the Sistine Ceiling, to more properly coincide with a contemporary pattern of vision: if the dull, "dirty," surfaces are unable to engage the eye, they should readjusted. Building façades should be shiny, the marble must appear fresh and new for modern sensibilities, regardless of when it was made. We are confident of our period's critical judgment as we are of its technical skills and its art.

Television modifies the entire population, the obese factory worker in Peoria and the anorexic junior high adolescent in Larchmont, not to mention the affluent bond trader who lives on Fifth Avenue and Seventy Second Street and who happens to be surrounded by Johns prints. The collector and his Vassar educated, fund-raiser wife are prone to go through the motions of tuning onto the educational channel for some tedious concert from Vienna, provided, that is, that no competing sporting event of specific relevance to childhood is being telecast. An old allegiance to the Yankees, the Jets, Syracuse University's basketball team, the Knicks or the Lakers definitely takes precedence. Even if these sporting events are themselves arrangements of their own kind, a residual zone of chance, of the unmanaged, the unmanipulated, of winning and of losing, of skill and showmanship, of fading in and fading out remains, leaving room for the release of stored fantasies.

The constant interruptions of the programs with commercials may also be apprehended as the repetitious battery of commercials interrupted by the program. The purpose of the entire TV viewing activity is not readily captured, producing another level of uneasiness that it shares with contemporary life and, of course, contemporary art. Sometimes the frustrated viewer seeks to avoid the repetitious ads by switching channels, click, click, to find another program; alas, the ever alert broadcasters have learned long ago to coordinate the presentation of their commercials on all the channels concurrently, frustrating the hunter who thinks he can escape paying his pound of flesh.

The inescapable breaks are interferences in a stream of logic, frustratingly broken, then rechanneled with equal abruptness, to be reopened again a few blinks later in an unending stream, like the sidewalks of the big city. Over the decades *entertainment interruptus* has become a normal mode of viewing, and perhaps even a comforting one because of its familiarity, like canned gravy. Comprehension has adapted itself around, or really incorporating, the obstacles. The constant pattern of amusement interspersed with advertising breaks represent severe, sometimes shocking shifts; after a period of time—weeks, months, years, decades—the procedure becomes the natural, expected and even desired mode of viewing. If altered, one might have to be weaned away (like stopping cigarette smoking) with yoga, acupuncture, or seminars.—TV Enders. Can such habits fail to affect ways of thinking and traditions of perception? To make the interruptions even more frustratingly disruptive, the breaks are traditionally programmed to coincide with high points in the action (suspenseful moments in a teleplay, for example) so that in order to have the prize, namely the unfolding of the story, one must swallow the commercials, in a technique inherited from radio. The Shadow knows. Skillful script writers automatically compose their texts with the proper breaks at the desired points along the length of the story. Something of the same framing is found in the news broadcasts and weather reports, structured so that tantalizing tidbits are suggested, then, smack!, the ad comes before a prediction of a tornado over the Hamptons. Nothing for nothing in this world, not even a decent flood, not to mention a rocket war.

Obesity has given rise to an entirely new network of enterprises that treat or are occupied with weight loss and weight control. In addition to the popular monthlies that inevitably feature new diets or at least refinements of old ones in every issue, more spectacular claims find their way into the weekly gossip newspapers—paradoxically distributed at the checkout counters of the supermarkets where most of the abusive shopping takes place—paving the way for the abusive eating that produces obesity. Along with dispatches about contact with the dead by someone usually connected with Elvis (Mario Lanza reincarnate?) whose post mortem legacy continues to exert a vise-like grip over the imagination of his generation and who was, after all, the gun-slinging subject of artistic multiples. In these publications one finds reports of inconceivably precocious births by seven–year–old girls in India or by old women well past the child-bearing age as if they were confirmations of miraculous births in the Bible; divorces and spicy heterosexual as well as homosexual affairs among the famous; along with elaborate horoscopes, predictions of calamities and reports about a man who lived through two electrocutions in the electric chair, Bermuda Triangle disappearances, and spottings of flying saucers and Big Foot. Another array of stories that recurs with monotonous frequency in these widely diffused gazettes centers upon claims of astonishing loss of weight in a brief time span.

Obviously these accounts aliment fantasies for sufferers (especially in outlying rural districts) who desperately cling to such eventualities even as they overload their huge shopping carriages. Four-and five-hundred pounders are reborn at one–third their maximum weight. Reality fades in and out as easily as turning channels on the Sony. In the same publications simplistic weight loss diets—

all cucumbers, all seaweed, all pasta, or as much ice cream as you want, that promise losses of 14 pounds the first week and a pound a day until the Last Judgment, are virtual fixed features.

Heavily patronized tested "scientific" programs have been organized across the nation in hospitals as well as by medical groups out of a deep-rooted tribal urgency and as a means of turning a healthy buck. Commercialized syndicates, beginning with Weight Watchers but with newer entrants in the field, have offered their services in the expanding marketplace for weight reduction. Perversely, I like to imagine a scenario in which the weight loss companies actually belong to the same conglomerates that also own those tobacco corporations whose portfolio includes fast food outlets, Seven-Elevens and the like. It is common knowledge that forswearing cigarette smoking usually is accompanied by a dramatic increase in appetite and a resultant rapid accumulation of pounds. The stuff out of which the weight is derived requires suppliers, especially of the easy-to-consume junk food one tends to nervously turn to under such conditions, which results two or three steps down the line in the demand for dietary weight loss programs.

Organizations offer courses lasting a fixed number of weeks that naturally can be renewed as long as one wishes, and the longer the better, lifetime membership the ideal. At the beginning of each session the wretched "student" has the embarrassing privilege of being weighed in like a prize fighter on which occasions he or she is publicly praised or cajoled in front of the peer group and when really successful obtain the admiration of the entire room of "overweighters", sometimes accompanied by spontaneous applause, like a winner at an asinine game show on TV who squeals with pleasure for a free week's vacation to Salt Lake City. Each school, as it were, has its own unique and recognizable style, its banner possibly designed by a Polish ex-freedom fighter, special logos, exclusive assumptions, public receptions, and its own track record, like an influential Fifty-Seventh Street art gallery who offers the shedding of ignorance instead of pounds, in keeping pace with the new.

Exactly how many billion pounds Weight Watchers have lost in the past two decades have never been publicly proclaimed but there must have been meteorites, and there must be a magical coefficient between them and the megatons of fatty hamburger meat sold. On the other hand, one is never sure how many times the client has lost the same pound, somewhat similar to the popular joke about a heavy smoker who when asked about the difficulty in stopping, replied that it was easy for him since he had done it dozens of times. We are ignorant of the total number of pounds shed by graduates of the Diet Centers across the nation last year but never as to how many Big Macs that were the instrument for amassing them in the first instance. All the plans to one extent or another are based on counting calories and on group hypnosis or at least strong group suggestion. Commonly held notions and aspirations about how unhealthy it is to be fat, how unsightly, and how depressed one is when overweight, are reinforced at the meetings. Even if one started out being reasonable content with being portly, after the constant harangues he becomes healthily despondent about his weight problem, too. Commitment is essential and the prime commitment, at least the one that most interests the sponsors, is the one to pay the weekly fee, which is the first step toward a resolve to be cured, something like the decision to pay the shrink, and the sacrifice is insurance that the program will be taken seriously. Put your money where your mouth is, but keep it closed.

Like stop-smoking clinics and seminars, and art appreciation sessions at leading museums, the diet programs have a hefty success rate over the short run. But over the longer haul, the pounds roll back in crushing waves. Fully aware of the blueprint, these same organizations will write and phone after a discrete span, inviting the "successful" and unsuccessful ex-clients alike back for a second and third round with the sure knowledge that many have fallen.

Another popular commercial approach to weight loss is treatment with drugs which usually involves ingesting hunger suppressants administered in conjunction with "water pills," that is, diuretics. Startling results can be obtained in a hurry among the just plain fat but not necessary the jumbos, who usually require surgery. On the other hand, the loss obtained in these cures is more provisional than the others, the weight tending to return with a vengeance upon the reemergence of old eating habits that were merely temporarily suppressed but never eradicated. The drugs, which are either purchased with a medical prescription or simply over the counter, implicate a range of possible side effects not the least of which is dependency but, additionally, personality deformations. Not uncommon after-effects include bulimia and anorexia nervosa, of which more will be said shortly. And when the weight comes back depression takes hold of the individual, provoking a profound downward spiral.

A popular self-administered treatment based upon a canned or boxed concoction is to be mixed with skimmed milk and consumed three times a day. The liquid contains all of the necessary nutrients one needs as well as the properly calculated number of calories to induce weight loss. Like all the other avenues, if it were followed to the letter, the desired results could be expected but when misunderstood and taken along with a regular food it can lead to significant weight gain.

Still another strategy for losing weight that may be conducted in combination with one of those approaches already specified is to pursue daily exercise programs. These may be undertaken under professional supervision in gyms, spas, pools and workout centers where instruction is available. Or they may be personally developed recipes which involve jogging, fast walking, biking on the road or stationary in front of the TV, rowing (usually with an expensive machine in a corner of the living room), or other exercise devices attached to the handle of the door, or wrapping an inflated plastic balloon around the midsection while gyrating for twenty minutes. They all work to the extent that calories are burned and they all involve an intensive investment—one absolutely needs special running shoes, for example, brightly colored flannel sweat suits designed by a chief international fashion house, apparel to be worn for their own sake as well as for exercise. Work out garb has progressed into status symbols of their own, signifying sporty, exercise-minded modern persons, someone who could easily collect neo-Barnet Newmans.

At the outset of a proper weight loss campaign, the elaborate collection of equipment and clothing is acquired but sooner or later, it is laid aside as utter apathy sets in, inevitably following a period of rote, minimalistic activities. The devices are first relegated to basements and attics to become prized items at garage sales across America's suburbs. Naturally the exercise industry is not exclusively oriented for weight loss, appealing also to those in the normal weight ranges for the sake of their hearts, lungs, body tone, bypass of one kind or another, and general appearance. But is there a more pitiful sight than watching a desperately overweight young woman in her late twenties, dressed in a modish cerulean blue workout clothes with matching pink and white Pumas, huffing and puffing down the paths of Riverside Park around 85th street, her lovely face distorted, knees aching, out of breath, hopefully holding out until the next meeting of the diet seminar a couple of miserable pounds the lighter?

An essential part of the paraphernalia for running is a Walkman hugging the ears, like the modern visitor to the mammoth citadel of art on Fifth Avenue where one can rent a kindred gadget that guides the innocent through the cultured corridors with dulcet instructions usually with a pompous English accent, native or acquired. The impersonalization of both activities operates to minimize social intercourse at every level imaginable. As a vehicle for assisting in the viewing of art, either of past or contemporary manifestations, the cassette invites the spectator only to absorb by means of banal information, but never to participate. One is presented with an authoritative though not necessarily intelligent explanation as if the tape is an unrivaled oracle of truth passed on as an act of mercy. Of course, we are habituated to participate in such a passive rapport in which, like television watching, the spectator is never invited to wonder, to challenge, to combat, or to reject. Who has enough courage to say that Guido Reni is a really a crashing bore or that Renoir painted hundreds of trite if not outright bad pictures along with some very fine ones? The only real alternative is to unplug, to switch channels, to fade out, to tune off.

The need for constant entertainment while engaged in other activities is typical of city life, where mostly young people have head phones for their home-made collections of tapes, the Stones or the Dead. It is a lonely business but by its very nature, the Walkman breeds further isolation, since chance encounters are difficult when sounds are funneled into the ears. Another popular gadget has the same net effect of increasing isolation: the oversized, portable jumbo ghetto boxes that blare out music that can be heard a block away. While unabashedly advertising their presence, announcing their mark as if creating aural graffiti, the result is thoroughly antisocial, compounded when riding around in an open car with the volume full blast.

Two aspects of the mechanism surrounding issues of obesity most relevant to the context of contemporary art are: (1) a dissatisfaction with one's appearance has been stirred up and then exploited to the benefit of an intricate web of commercial activities; and (2) aesthetic assumptions that lie behind the public attitude towards the appearance of being fat have been perpetuated. Issues of taste, style, perception, fashions, and reception are closely linked with obesity and its opposite, anorexia.

Bulimia and Anorexia Nervosa

The fear of fatness has husbanded extreme reactions in terms of eating habits that, in turn, have effected the appearance and health of a substantial minority of the population in the United States, particularly among young women. Anorexia nervosa and bulimia, like obesity, are aligned to processes of perception and reception of the world beyond the individual, especially as related to aspects of self perception. These diseases have been studied extensively by medical researchers and psychologists but have been subjected to relatively little analysis by social scientists, although they are surely social in genesis, the result of forces bound in the social order, accentuated and reinforced by a heartless and soulless mass media. Hence, the grueling cure has a low rate of success. The fear of fatness among those suffering from anorexia nervosa and its sister bulimia is an obsessive phobia that occupies the largest portion of the sufferer's day. Mainly found among adolescent girls, cases occur in all age groups and in both sexes, although women outnumber men to such an extent that it is often thought of as a woman's illness. Instances have been interpreted as having occurred in the Middle Ages among spiritual women saints who went virtually without eating for years at a time. Nonetheless, the disease for all practical purposes is a modern one, corresponding - at least temporally - with the contemporary art of the past generation or so.

Those young people who suffer from anorexia nervosa have taken the social pressure against appearing obese as an obsession. The purpose of their lives seems to revolve around the subject of food, much like the obese. They are often fixated gourmet cooks, whose anomalous behavior is such that they will not even eat the delicious foods they themselves prepare. Immense energy is expended in controlling or layering over hunger to such an extent that near total denial takes over. They lose track not only of their physical appearance which, once the disease seizes control, is inevitably emaciated, but have a spurious estimate of their body size. Bodily functions become altered as well. For example, as the disease wins out, their gastric physiology apparently gives signals of fullness when in fact the intestinal track is virtually empty. A few sentences cannot pretend to satisfactorily sum up even basic notions connected with this puzzling and complex illness, for which cures have been elusive. Once the mechanism has been set in motion, fundamental attitudes toward reality and even of self-preservation have been deformed to such an extent that many suffering of anorexia nervosa actually die of starvation. It seems to me that it represents the maximum Dada act, and since so much of the art of the past generation might be interpreted as Dada revival or survival, the relevance becomes increasingly obvious. In the land of plenty, coming from family environments that are well-to-do, these young people, in particular, offer the most total rejection of their world possible.

In the course of their affliction, anorexics, who are known to be perfectionists and overachievers, tensely under control, extremely sensitive to criticism, gradually lose their capabilities due to malnutrition. They dress in a mode aimed to conceal their concentration camp appearance for as long as possible. The young women after a year or two no longer experience menses, hair begins to grow all over the body, and sexual urges, following an early phase of increased activity, decline dramatically. That as many as 10 percent of college women suffer from anorexia nervosa or the connected disease, bulimia, persons who come from the relatively well-educated portion of the society, is a statistic of astonishing value in measuring the mood of contemporary life.

The bulimics, who belong to the same category and social strata, tend to binge, eating, more often than not alone, colossal quantities of food, an apparent need that may have been induced by stress. Like the anorexic, their fear of getting fat is so intense that after "pigging out" they self induce vomiting as a means of removing the potential fat producing foods from their systems. Often they also make use of strong purges as do anorexics for the same goals, so that they expel the food from both ends of the digestive track at the same time. Unlike anorexics bulimics may be of relatively average weight but their behavioral patterns and their modes of perception are equally distorted: stealing, sexual promiscuity, and lying are common. They may, for example, consume so much food that their entire digestive track is as hard as a compacted trash bundle, causing them agonizing pain. It is primarily a private, secretive activity and the bulimic assiduously seeks to hide the motif of gobbling food. The bulimic will quietly excuse himself/herself when in company, discharge into the toilet bowl, and return to eating. The constant regurgitation induces sundry health problems, including painful digestive tracks, kidney ailments, lung disorders and premature tooth decay, in a paradigm of self induced injury comparable to the battering induced in other social situations common in modern society.

What we see then in the case of the obese, the anorexic and the bulimic is a configuration of severe distortion of reality and the inability to insert themselves in the world. Everything seems to be an exaggeration, either too much or too little. Dimensions are completely out of proportion. The sufferers may be said to share distorted visions with their contemporaries: a sixty-foot yellow and red mobile, a black on black painting the length of an airplane hanger, a three story orange carrot, or on the opposite end of the continuum, the tiny repetitions of nail heads, hundreds of them, maybe thousands, hammered with painstaking precision to form an aimless constellation.

The Tyranny of the Detail

A generation ago, Kenneth Clark prepared a "picture book," offering his favorite details from paintings of the past. The validation of the status the detail holds for the art viewing public with such an authoritative pedigree has to be regarded as indicative. Probably since the beginning of painting, when man first etched his shadow on the bare ground with a stick or imagery was sighted in the flames of the hearth, attention must have been drawn to discrete particulars in preference to others within a pictorial environment. We can readily reconstruct a tale in which a cave dweller pointed out to an open-eyed child one or another feature of a hunt depicted on his wall. Greek painting on curved surfaces of a vase can only be read in fixed segments, those visible at one unit of time beyond which either the object or the spectator must turn. In more recent times, details from known and even famous objects often have been portrayed through graphics. The propensity for illustrating art and specific details thrived with the advent of photography. Especially in the past thirty or forty years the phenomenon has transformed itself into one of the most

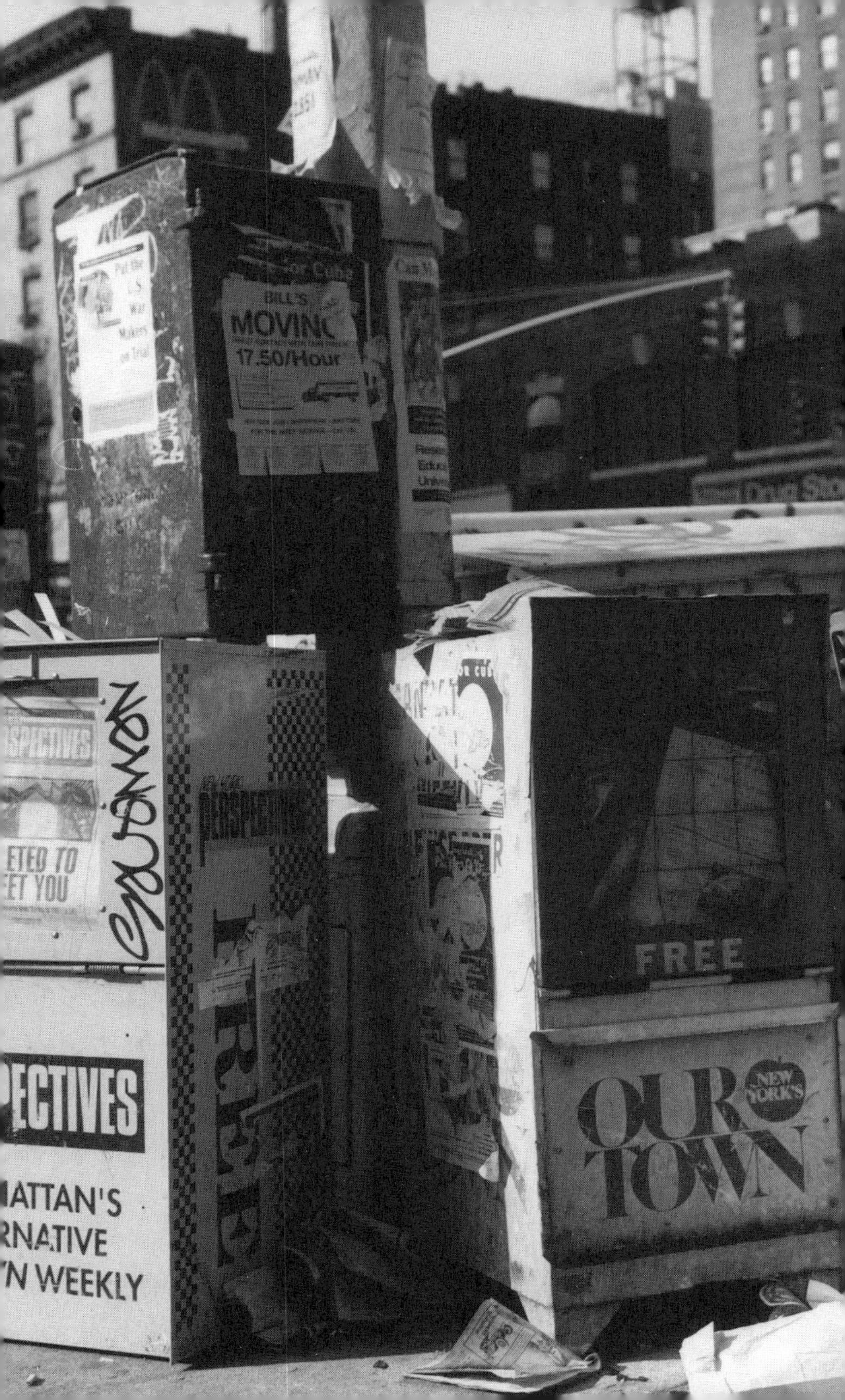
Put the
U.S.
War
Makers
on Trial
BILL'S
MOVING
17.50/Hour
PERSPECTIVES
ETED TO
ET YOU
ECTIVES
ATTAN'S
RNATIVE
N WEEKLY
PERSPECTIVES
FREE
OUR
TOWN
NEW
YORK'S

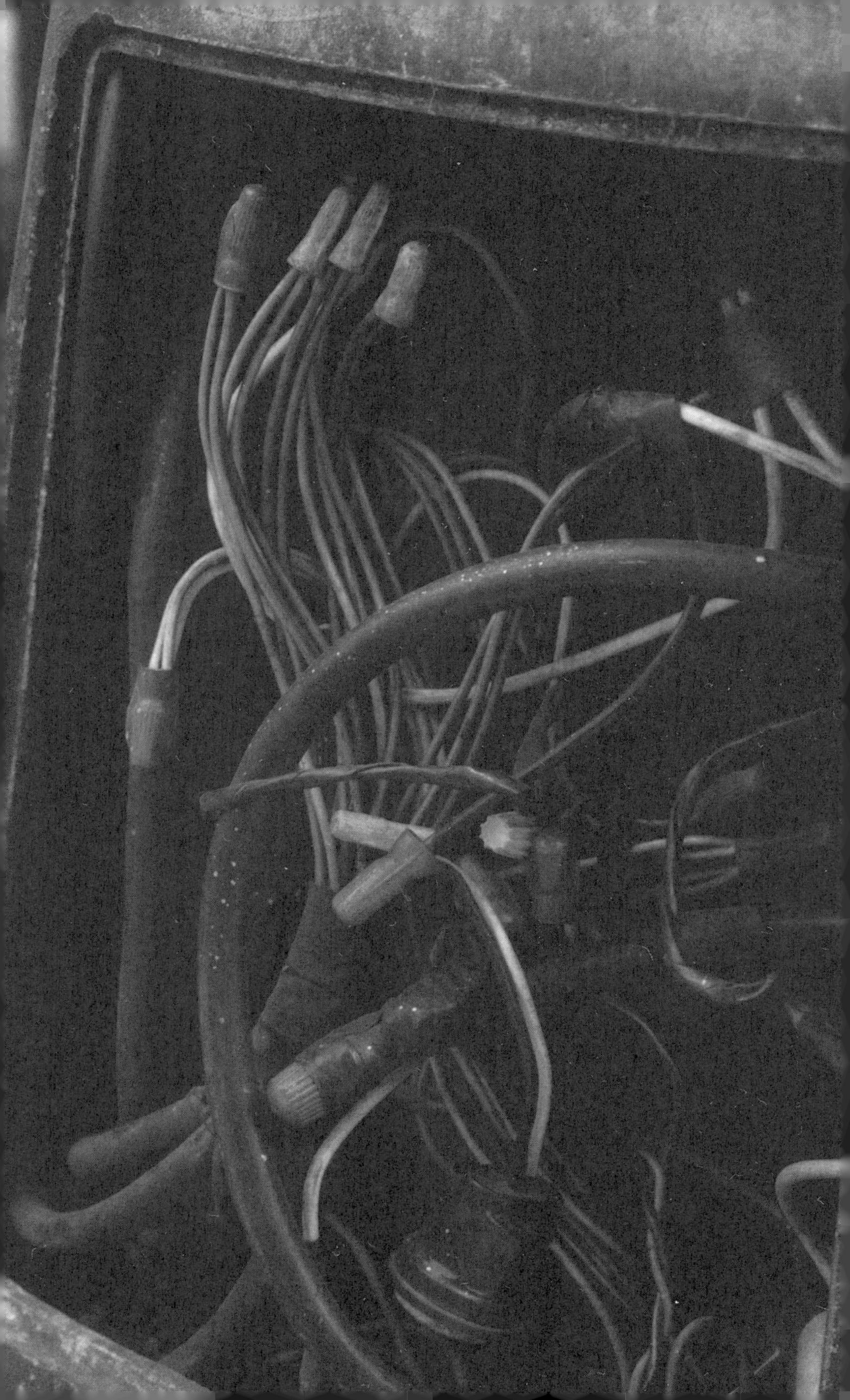

characteristic aspects of vision. Furthermore, the process has evolved into an indispensable tool for analyzing almost anything, from a layer of cancerous tissue to the surface of a famous painting. And, as I shall suggest, the detail has become a commanding factor in the conception and creation of new art.

With the introduction of opulently illustrated art books, monographic assemblages, themselves artificial processes that require exclusive exegeses all their own, the stage had been set for the possibility of becoming acquainted with a vast, veritably endless aggregate of objects and artifacts from every culture imaginable and from all epochs, merely by flipping the pages of a Skira or Phaidon volume. Today the picture book industry is, if anything, more active that ever. A subtle change may be detected abuilding, however. The reproduction of details in an earlier time was normally predicated upon the recognition, surely unstated, of the indivisibility of the totality from which it was lifted. With advances in printing techniques especially in the now nearly universal application of color, the richly hued detail has frequently and almost inevitably become confused with the whole entity. That is to say, the fragment has become an independent, expressive unit standing all by itself. This, despite the well recognized reality that it has never been possible to effectively "read" a picture in its wholeness. A process of electing cherished points of attraction intervened, although a final step was inevitably implied. A mental synthesis has to occur in the brain. As we concentrate on a single object whether in nature, as in a still life, or in a painting of a still life, we cannot focus exclusively on one portion or another without distorting the objects surrounding it, much less those at greater distance from the central cone of concentration. In other words, fragmentation was always operative, as is confirmed when reading a selected passage of a Titian, Monet, or Seurat in which the dots and strokes are integrated by the mind into a signifying passage.

One might approach the argument by harboring the generalized proposition that while in the past the tendency to harmonize and unify prevailed, in the contemporary situation, the fragmentation is left fragmented and even sought. Nor is there a desire, will, or necessity for synthesis. Indeed the fragment becomes the entirety, and conversely the whole is fully subverted.

The frenzied proliferation of pictorial imagery that bombards the modern individual is readily confirmed. Periodical publications with jumbo circulations, including daily newspapers, not to mention films and television, have promoted the normalization of the fragmentation process. The teaching of art history and art appreciation is intrinsically predicated on the detail, in a methodology compounded by the insidious practice of unrelenting comparisons. Two details, if not entire compositions, are laid out side by side on bright, flickering screens. Consequently they appear to be the same size regardless of the original dimensions; then, profound conclusions are drawn with alchemical wizardry about influences, exchanges, "borrowings," and transformations. The pattern is drastically distant from the avenues by which artists conceived in the past and do today, even when they are experiencing an "influence." Whatever are the ways, they are never the one-to-one match up, even in the case of the most droll inventors.

A vast separation persists between the routine of isolating a detail for concentration while observing the entire picture or sculpture in a museum, gallery, public space, or even in the studio of the artist, and being presented with the detail without the whole, mechanically extrapolated from its contexts, in an accidentally achieved scale. Boxed in and enframed by the conventionalized rectangularity demanded of the process, details have become an essential component of the habit of seeing. But do we ever really read sections of a painting in squared off segments anyway? I suggest not: instead, our sights bounce into and around a favored or particularly engaging section, one that has no fixed boundaries at all. Our assessment of specific, charged portions fade from one or another section of a picture and then fade out again, slipping and sliding through the blurred, shifting edges. To repeat, the details found in every book on art as well as in the public media create an arbitrary, artificial experience, detached from actual perception, and have accrued their own rules. On the other hand, the detail has achieved a disproportionately intense impact upon even routine vision.

Before proceeding along this line of argumentation, several related situations need to be brought into the discourse. The telescopic camera lens, for example, renders the world in bits and pieces with a fragmentary and often unreal (surreal?) flavor. Related is the application of the close-up, an essential ingredient in the vocabulary of artistic photography and, in particular, in film-making. In turn, the close-up has formed a compelling experience for the conception as well as the reception of modern art,

one we seek at all costs to avoid on the broad
avenue near the great university.

The utilization of the close-up is even more
insistent for television than for feature films due to
the smaller format, for which a whole figure,
configuration of figures, wide vistas, mountain
ranges, a stadium bursting with anxious sport fans
clutching their beer cans, is never as effective as
centering upon a distinctive individual, perhaps an
overfed coach or a smiling "pretty" girl. Diversely,
with large–screen films the details are exploited
within self-conscious juxtapositions. In contrast,
for television broadcasting the detail or close-up
functions as a consummate vehicle for what is
conveyed. Advertising art found in mass media
publications also reveals a penchant for the detail,
presumably for its inherent immediate impact.
Gradual, measured reflection of complex whole
views is almost regularly passed over in favor of a
whack on the head. The fragmentation may be
achieved by selection from the larger
photographic representation on the basis of what
is perceived to be effective for printing, or the
selectivity may be the result of the photographer's
insights from the start. What all this means is that
we have become unremittingly habituated to
seeing the world in sub-units, in snippets. Even in
images of ourselves our entire bodies have given
way to views not even of the head but only the
face. (Parenthetically, at least one reasonably
well-known contemporary painter has spent
virtually his entire artistic life representing aspects
of his own imagined, close–up, enlargements.)
Reality, in fact, has become conditioned by the
repeatedly reinforced awareness of these
segments, irrationally bisected by designers and
art directors, and equally irrationally arranged, one
with another. By definition, the "effectiveness" of

any specific image, but especially the detail, is almost exclusively the motive behind the inclusion or rejection in the media. A comprehensive totality has become an irrelevancy: rather, the infinite subdivisions, the configured segments have taken command. One may vainly try to fit the myriad excerpts together like a puzzle to achieve a sensible whole, but only with enormous effort, due to leaps in scale, color, tone, and with little hope of success. The fact remains, few bother. More likely they are never unified. The concept of a whole has become—and here we are getting close to my main point—hazy, irrelevant, and ultimately expendable.

Reproducibility and Detailability

It is common knowledge among artists that the quality of a particular work does not necessary emerge in reproduction. Or putting it differently, certain works reproduce well, regardless of their inherent quality, others do not. This realization leads to the general question of reproducibility. Over time, one has to begin to wonder whether art objects are conceived for their own sake or, and of course I am assuming that this happens unconsciously, for the potential impact they may inspire via reproductions. In the second instance the media dictates artistic events. The inclusion of letters, ditties, poems, sayings, word fragments which can be easily spotted and read in reproduction are a common ingredient of contemporary art, leading one to wonder if their reproducibility was not a factor in their creation.

In a parallel situation, modern restoration of painting and sculpture, in particular, may be affected by similar conditions. Often sponsored by individual corporations of entities who use the results of the interventions they have paid for in their advertising, the success or failure can be weighted not so much by how the object actually appears, but how it appears in reproduction, to the wide world. Hence the kind of restoration, the extent to which changes are made in the object, and the kind of changes may be dictated by the reproducibility quotient.

The thrust of my point here is to suggest that contemporary art has expanded the previous boundaries in its awareness of reproducibility and with it the potentialities for the guided selection of details. We might call this second condition, *detailability.* One would have to be a thoroughgoing cynic to suggest that artists include elements in their collages, say, photographic slivers, that can be reproduced with unique effect and may be singled out from time to time for the glamorous blown-up detail in a prestigious publication. Yet, the process of mass media reproductions are such that inevitably an effect filtered onto the art has to be assumed.

To return to the question of the effect of the detail upon modern creativity and modern reception, I suggest that many "complete" works of recent creation may be understood as "details" which have transformed themselves to wholes of their own. In fact, to carry the notion a step further, much of contemporary art is detail. A new species of wholeness has been achieved, one that has been heavily impacted by the processes mentioned above. The habits formed by regularly leafing through the pages of an art book or monthly art magazine, rapidly glancing at illustrations in the more popular publications, as well as the process with which one tends to move in a museum, or still more pertinently in an art gallery, when viewing a one-person show, demand engaging images, to induce even a brief pause by a potential viewer. Given the orientation of vivid imagery on the television screen in conjunction with the obvious impact of advertising art on their vigorous details and striking close ups, if a contemporary painting cannot attract attention and maintain it, the work is liable to be mercilessly passed over, totally ignored. Due to the vast competition for visual attention, especially as we tend to be increasingly immersed in a city environment and consequently further removed from an idyllic nature, the art object must win a sympathetic reception, a favorable first impression, before any expectation for deeper critical communication can be expected, if that is even possible. Otherwise we can click it off, fade it out and rip open another Snickers, reach out for Mars or far beyond for the Milky Way.

James Beck is the author of ten books on Italian Renaissance painting and sculpture, and scores of articles and essays on similar subjects, as well as on modern and contemporary art. Beck has a PhD from Columbia University, where he has taught the history of art for the past 30 years. He studied in Italy and the United States, specializing in painting, sculpture and drawing.

Among his most important books are a monograph on Raphael (Abrams), an overview of Italian Renaissance painting (Harper) and *Leonardo's Rules of Painting: An Unconventional Approach to Modern Art* (Viking). His two-volume study of the Sienese sculptor Jacopo della Quercia (Columbia University Press) was published in January 1992.

A leader in the movement to halt the over-restoration of artworks, Beck has been an outspoken critic of the cleaning of Michelangelo's Sistine Chapel ceiling.

Beck has held a number of prestigious awards, among them a Guggenheim Fellowship and a Senior Fellowship from the National Endowment for the Humanities. He recently completed a six-year term as Chair of the Art History Department at Columbia University and is currently at work on a book recounting his criminal trial for aggravated defamation, brought against him by an Italian art restorer.

He is the founder and executive director of *ArtWatch International*, a not-for-profit organization concerned with the preservation of the cultural heritage.

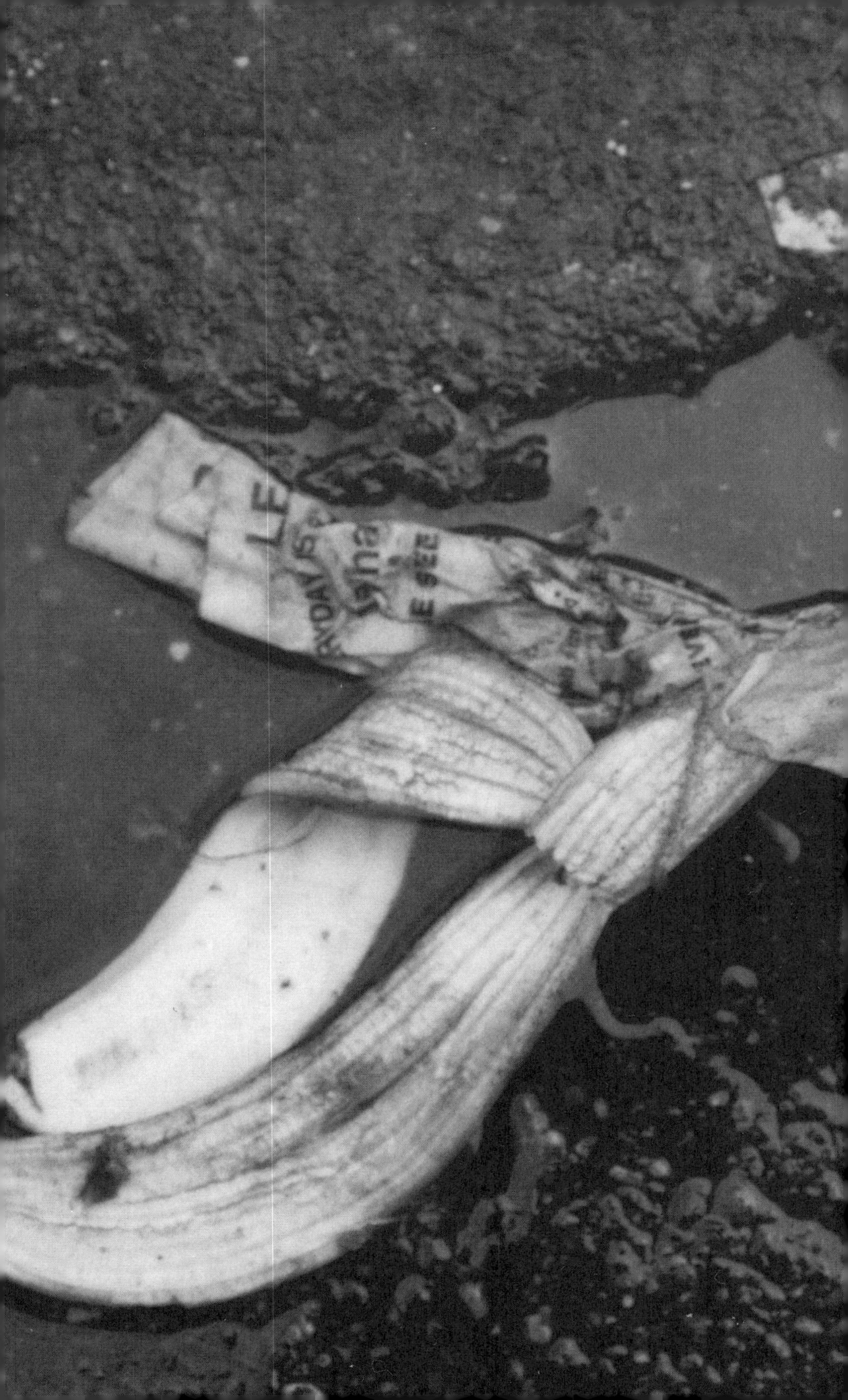

OREO
OREO
SANDWICH COOKIES
NET WT 1½ OZ